2001:
A Developmental Odyssey

Jeanne L. Higbee, Editor
Dana Britt Lundell, Associate Editor
Irene M. Duranczyk, Associate Editor

Devjani Banerjee-Stevens, Assistant Editor

Table of Contents

Editorial Board iv

Foreword v
    Linda R. Thompson

Introduction 1
    Jeanne L. Higbee

Implementing a Learning Framework Course 3
    Russell B. Hodges, Carol W. Dochen, & De C. Sellers

When ESL is Developmental:
A Model Program for the Freshman Year 15
    Robin Murie & Renata Thomson

Narrative Therapy and College Basic Writers 29
    Mary P. Deming

Developing Writers Using Technology 47
    Patsy Krech

Stigma 53
    Mark Pedelty

Developmental Education and Alfred Binet:
The Original Purpose of Standardized Testing 71
    Patrick R. Perdew

The Relationship Between Concept of Intelligence and Teacher Goals 87
    Linda Maitland

Practical Approaches to Using Learning Styles in Higher Education 105
    Dunn, R. & Griggs, S.A. (Eds.), reviewed by Martha Maxwell

Call for Submissions 107

Guidelines for Authors 108

Editorial Board

Foreward

Dear Colleagues:

I am delighted to introduce to you the 2001 NADE Monograph, aptly titled *2001: A Developmental Odyssey*. This monograph comes to you as a benefit of your membership in NADE and reflects the variety and depth of the types of activity and research our association members engage in.

The field of developmental education has been on an odyssey to open accessibility to a broad spectrum of individuals since Harvard first reserved places in its student body for students from working class families in the 17th century. That the odyssey continues into the 21st century is evident in this excellent compendium of essays researched and written by your colleagues—professionals within the National Association for Developmental Education.

I would like to extend a heartfelt "thank you" to Jeanne Higbee, editor, to Dana Lundell and Irene Duranczyk, associate editors, and to Devjani Banerjee-Stevens, assistant editor, for their dedication to this project and for the many, many hours they have volunteered to bring it to you in the form you now see. Without the commitment of these professionals, as well as the writers of the chapters you are about to read–and the many other writers who submitted articles–this monograph would not be possible.

NADE's monograph series represents not only an opportunity for you to read articles by seasoned professionals in the field, but also for your voice to be heard about the aspects of developmental education that are important to you. Guidelines for authors are included at the back of this monograph. Consider submitting an article for next year's issue!

Now, I invite you to sit down, open the following pages and join your colleagues in . . . A Developmental Odyssey . . .

Linda R. Thompson
President, National Association for Developmental Education
2000-2001

Introduction

Jeanne L. Higbee
University of Minnesota

Editor

This is perhaps the most controversial volume in the National Association for Developmental Education (NADE) monograph series to date. I credit our outstanding editorial board members for their diligence in reviewing these manuscripts. Their constructive feedback assisted chapter authors and the editorial staff in developing a monograph that features several of the most difficult issues in the field today. This volume does not focus on some of the traditional topics for developmental education publications. Instead it addresses pedagogical and administrative practices that will continue to play an important role as the profession redefines itself in the new millennium.

The first chapter, by Hodges, Dochen, and Sellers, provides the theoretical perspective and specific suggestions for "Implementing a Learning Framework Course." These courses, based on cognitive theory, teach learning strategies in a manner that encourages students to become independent learners. Similarly, the next chapter, by Murie and Thomson, describes a model to facilitate students who are non-native speakers of English in becoming autonomous learners in an American higher education setting. In the third chapter of this monograph, Deming explores how students can address issues affecting their lives through narrative therapy, a constructive tool for basic writers. Then, in chapter four, Krech relates how she uses technology in the teaching of writing.

In the next chapter, Pedelty follows up on an issue that has been articulated by developmental educators for decades, but has just recently begun surfacing in the literature in the field. Pedelty opens the door for further discussion of the question of stigma as it relates to developmental education programs, students, faculty and staff, and the profession as a whole. Perdew provides further insights as he describes Binet's original goals in the development of standardized tests, and how these tests subsequently have been used to label individuals and groups. Perdew asserts that developmental educators use standardized tests for the purpose for which they were designed, to assess individual student needs in order to assist students in adopting appropriate learning strategies so that they can develop to their full potential. Perhaps Perdew gives our profession too much credit. I fear that within the field of developmental education, we still misuse standardized tests, sometimes as the only factor considered in the placement, grouping, and final outcomes assessment of our students. Hopefully, Perdew's essay will prompt further research and discussion of the policies and practices (the theme of the 2002 monograph) related to the use of standardized testing in developmental education. Finally, Maitland's chapter sheds further light on the concept of intelligence as applied to teaching.

This volume concludes with Martha Maxwell's review of *Practical Approaches to Using Learning Styles in Higher Education* by Dunn and Griggs. I am indebted to Martha for her annual contribution to the NADE monograph series. Her book reviews have been instrumental in guiding developmental educators to worthwhile reading to enhance professional development.

As always, I want to express my appreciation to the members of the NADE executive board for their continued support, and particularly to Linda Thompson, NADE president, for assisting in the selection of the theme for this year's monograph. In this transition year following Pat Dwinell's retirement, I also thank Dana Lundell and Irene Duranczyk, associate editors, and Devjani Banerjee-Stevens, assistant editor, for their many contributions to this project.

Implementing a Learning Framework Course

Russell B. Hodges & Carol W. Dochen
Southwest Texas State University

De C. Sellers
Episcopal Theological Seminary of the Southwest

Abstract

Learning framework courses represent the most recent manifestation of American higher education's efforts to help undergraduate students become academically successful. These courses integrate theory and practice from a diverse array of educational and psychological theories, and the courses are increasingly successful in helping students achieve academic goals and persist to graduation. This chapter describes the evolution of such a course developed at a four-year, regional, public, postsecondary institution, from its beginnings as a traditional study skills course in 1973 through its current status as a model for other institutions that want to increase the academic success and retention of their students.

For additional information contact: Russell B. Hodges • Southwest Texas State University • College of Education • 601 University Drive • San Marcos, TX • e-mail: RH12@swt.edu

S tudy skills and college reading courses have shared a common history in American higher education as the birth of this field began with a reading improvement experiment designed for college students in 1894 (Stahl, Hynd, & Henk, 1986). Colleges have formally focused on teaching students the rituals of college study since the 1920s (Maxwell, 1997), and through most of the century, study skills content was an integral part of remedial reading courses or was taught separately in remedial study skills courses or as noncredit mini-courses. However, the pedagogy of simply teaching students specific skills such as a notetaking, reading, or time management systems began to erode in the late 1970s and was replaced by numerous academic

Figure 1. Matrix of Academic Success Courses

Course Type & Typical Credits	Definition	Sample Topics	Study Methods Taught
Orientation (Where/ What) 1-credit	Overview of resources and services	Student services on campus, financial aid, library tours	Where to study on campus
Navigation (How) 1-3 credits	How and when to use a variety of resources and facilities	How and when to meet with an advisor/ faculty member. How to fill out financial aid forms	Developing time management plans and goals for studying
Academic & Personal Development (Transition) 1-3 credits	Facilitates students' transition into college; focus on adjustment issues	Homesickness, roommates, career development, independence, stress management	Differences between studying in high school and college, stress management, independence
Academic Skills (Study Skills) 3-credits	Helps students develop academic skills and habits related to locating and recording information	Time management, listening to lectures, note taking, study groups, test taking	How to take notes or tips for studying effectively in groups
Learning to Learn (Learning Strategies) 3-credits	Courses which facilitate students' abilities to understand and retain material	Mnemonics, SQ3R, concept mapping, annotating texts, learning styles	Development of learning strategies for use during individual and group study
Critical Thinking (Independent Thinking) 3-credits	Promote the evaluation of and independent thought	Evaluation, organization, recognizing errors in thinking, application of problem solving, debate	Information about studying might focus on the development of critical thinking strategies such as evaluating evidence
Learning Framework (Theoretical perspective of knowledge acquisition) 3 credits	Fosters students' abilities to monitor and regulate their own learning through an understanding of themselves as learners	Self regulated learning, strategic learning, information processing, methods of inquiry	Student's ability to independently create an environment conducive to learning using a repertoire of appropriate learning and monitoring strategies

Note. From "An In-depth Look at Academic Success Courses," by R. P. Cole, C. Babcock , E. T. Goetz, and C. E. Weinstein, 1997. Paper presented at the meeting of the College Reading and Learning Association, Sacramento, CA. Adapted with permission from the authors.

support classes with such titles as Orientation, Learning Strategies, Effective Learning, Creative Learning, Freshman Seminar, and Strategic Learning. Confusion exists in understanding the purpose and determining the academic rigor of these various academic success course models. Researchers have attempted to differentiate academic success courses by assessing syllabi and textbooks and surveying faculty members involved in teaching these courses across the country. Cole, Babcock, Goetz, and Weinstein (1997) created a matrix to classify academic success courses. The matrix begins with those courses that focus on lower-level skills and topics, such as a one-credit hour orientation course that provides students with an overview of their postsecondary institution, and ends with a three-credit hour learning framework course steeped in cognitive theory and learning strategies. These learning framework courses have the avowed purpose of teaching students to become independent learners.

A synopsis of each course type follows; however, Figure 1 provides a more extensive overview. Orientation courses provide students with a comprehensive overview of university resources and facilities. Navigation courses teach students how and when to use a variety of university resources and facilities. Academic and Personal Development courses facilitate students' transition from high school into the university environment by focusing on adjustment to college. Academic Skills courses help students develop good academic habits and study skills. Learning to Learn courses facilitate students' abilities to understand and retain course material as well as provide instruction in study skills. Some courses integrate low-level theory into their content. Critical Thinking courses promote the evaluation of independent thought and decision-making processes. Learning Framework courses foster students' abilities to monitor and regulate their own learning through the development of a perspective about themselves as learners. Theories from cognitive and behavioral psychology are deeply rooted into the course curriculum (Cole et al., 1997).

Definition of a Learning Framework Course

The hallmark of a learning framework course is the presentation of theoretical models as the curricular core (Cole et al., 1997). Although such courses do teach study skills and learning strategies as applications, those skills are taught at a sophisticated, reflective, individualized level—a level characteristic of collegiate learning. In contrast, study skills courses teach students specific and simplified study techniques and methods where the focus is on the acquisition of the skill, not the comprehension of why and how human learning can be enhanced. Study skills topics include instruction in time management, notetaking, textbook study methods, strategies for preparing and taking examinations, and strategies in memory and concentration. Other topics include units on research paper writing, career planning, adapting to academic regulations, and improving personal and social adjustment to college (Maxwell, 1997).

By comparison, learning framework courses teach students the process of collegiate learning (i.e., cognitive skills); the focus is on the comprehension of human learning based on current theories. Students then develop individualistic learning strategies based on their knowledge of these theoretical underpinnings. Learning framework courses integrate cognitive psychology theory with learning strategies in order that students will understand the reasons for engaging in specific study behaviors and how to adapt to differing circumstances. For instance, information processing models help students understand the elaborate set of internal or cognitive processes involved in the acquisition and organization of knowledge. Learning framework courses have strong academic content with a solid foundation in research and theory.

One example of a learning framework course has been offered since 1977 at the University of Texas at Austin (UT-Austin). Claire Ellen Weinstein, co-author of the *Learning and Study Strategies Inventory* (Weinstein, Palmer, & Schulte, 1987), has led the field in developing a learning framework course. Weinstein's course was recently cited as one of five innovative alternative approaches to developmental education (Boylan, 1999). The course, titled "Educational Psychology: Individual Learning Skills (EDP 310)" is a three-credit hour undergraduate course taken for a grade. It is not required for any degree program and is considered a free elective. EDP 310 targets students who enter the university under special circumstances or who experience academic difficulty after reentry. Instructors are advanced graduate students in educational psychology who receive extensive, continuous training. The course content is driven by Weinstein's Model of Strategic Learning, a model inspired by systems theory and Gestalt psychology (Weinstein, Dierking, Husman, Roska, & Powdrill, 1998). The model emphasizes how students learn in specific academic environments and is presented as a series of four major components: skill, will, self-regulation, and the academic environment.

Weinstein attributes much of her inspiration in developing the strategic learning model to the earlier work by Wilbert J. McKeachie, from the University of Michigan, and his research on strategic teaching (Weinstein, 1994). McKeachie and his colleagues have developed a four-credit hour introductory cognitive psychology course titled "Learning to Learn." The goal of the course is to help students develop efficient learning strategies and become life-long learners (Pintrich, McKeachie, & Lin, 1987). Learning to Learn, first taught in 1982, provides instruction in theory and research in cognitive psychology and in the application of learning strategies for studying. Topics covered include learning for lectures, texts, and discussions; memory models and strategies; motivation; writing skills; test-taking strategies; problem solving; and self-management. Research on the effectiveness of Learning to Learn found significant changes in students' self-reports of learning strategies and small changes in students' grade point averages (Pintrich et al.).

A third learning framework course, "Educational Psychology 1350: Effective Learning (EDP 1350)" of Southwest Texas State University (SWT), represents a classic evolution from a traditional study skills course to a fully integrated learning framework course. The remainder of this chapter will review its history, current curriculum, student population, and retention outcomes. A final section will comment on the new statewide funding policies in Texas for learning framework courses.

Evolution of a Model Learning Framework Course

In 1973, SWT hired an educational specialist to create a psychology course to enhance students' academic success. This traditional study skills course had both a classroom and a laboratory experience. As EDP 1350 migrated from the traditional format to a learning framework course over the next 30 years, the laboratory component of the course evolved into a multi-faceted learning assistance center, which is funded by state appropriations and student fees. The center provides free individual, group, and online peer tutoring for most freshman and sophomore courses, with the greatest demand in mathematics, accounting, English, and the natural sciences. The center also provides Supplemental Instruction (SI) and study skills workshops. The center's holistic philosophy trains tutors to instruct students in learning and study strategies in addition to content skills. The director of the course also coordinated the early development of the learning center's program, and many tutors from the center have served as undergraduate facilitators for the course. Students needing more instruction in learning skills and strategies often have been referred to the course by the tutors. The synergy of the simultaneous development of two coordinated programs energized the creativity of each one.

The course was first offered in the psychology department, and the early curriculum was similar to that of many college reading and study skills courses originating in the early 1970s. The focus was on improving students' reading comprehension, vocabulary, notetaking, time management, and test-taking skills. At the end of the semester, the students evaluated their accomplishments and goals in a written self-evaluation. The course used projects and papers as the basis for grading, and much class time was devoted to practice exercises. Theory was rarely a topic. In the years that followed, the wide diversity of faculty members, many with extensive backgrounds in psychology and education, transformed the course into an applied learning and behavior management skills course that offers students both current learning theory and research applications. Some of the hallmark changes included: content tests as 30 to 50% of the grade, strict attendance and late paper policies, and cognitive behavior modification theory and practice. Grading standards increasingly became congruent with the normal undergraduate grading standards in the liberal arts and the social sciences. At the annual curriculum conferences, faculty agonized over the array of required subjects as new topics were added and old topics discarded.

An important dichotomy emerged. Theories crept into the curriculum: first, those stressing cognitive behavior modification, then cognitive and moral development in adults, and finally information processing. A concurrent development was the faculty's conviction that the course must be a realistic laboratory experience; that is, students must be accountable for their academic behaviors. Thus, attendance and timeliness of assignments were rewarded. Syllabi were especially specific in the required behavioral demands on students. Faculty extensively used behavioral counseling techniques to help students accept the responsibility for their actions and modify their academic behaviors, if necessary.

Currently, EDP 1350 is offered through the department of Educational Administration and Psychological Services within the College of Education at SWT. The course enrolls approximately 500 to 600 students throughout the academic year. Class enrollment is limited to 30 students per section. Usually 10 sections are offered each fall and spring semester, and one or two sections are offered each summer term. What has evolved over almost a 30-year period is a four-part curriculum model for the course, which consists of self-assessment, self-regulation, cognitive theories and strategies, and self-change. The curriculum enables students to develop effective learning skills and strategies that offer maximal opportunities for them to transfer and apply learning skills and strategies across many academic courses and programs. The model integrates theory and practice throughout the course. Every element of the course—readings, lectures, discussions, directed group activities, assignments, projects, and tests—illustrates a carefully planned sequence that leads students toward a thoughtful, self-sufficient mode of academic behaviors.

Self-assessment, the first unit of the course, helps students formulate a clear portrait of themselves as learners by having them complete self-assessment inventories and then use the data from each to deepen understanding of their learning strengths and weaknesses. Weinstein's *Learning and Study Strategies Inventory* (Weinstein et al., 1987) assists students in assessing their preferred learning strategies. Kolb's *Learning Styles Inventory* (Kolb, 1999), based on his theory of experiential learning, introduces students to the concept of differing learning preferences. The *Myers-Briggs Type Indicator Form M* (Briggs & Myers, 1998) illustrates how personality type directly influences values, decisions, communication, and learning preferences. The introduction of multiple intelligence theory (Gardner, 1993) allows students to develop a more comprehensive view of their own abilities. Students also evaluate their own skills in reading, writing, critical thinking, and mathematics.

Self-regulation, the second part of the course, is a way of approaching academic tasks through experience and self-reflection. Students develop a greater awareness of their own behavior, motivation, and academic learning. Students come to understand self-regulation (Pintrich, 1995) by setting achievement goals, using self-monitoring techniques, investigating their motivation, and using principles of self-discipline and time planning. Motivation theories introduced in the course include Maslow's (1970) Theory of Motivation and Weiner's (1986) Attribution Theory. Students also study Perry's (1968) theory on how intellectual and moral values develop and the implications such development has on how adults study and learn. Two particularly important concepts are self-discipline (Peck, 1978) and self-esteem (Branden, 1994), especially the deliberate development of self-efficacy (Bandura, 1993).

Cognitive theory and strategies are the focus of the third section of the course. An information-processing model of adult college learning (Gagné, Yekovich, & Yekovich, 1993) is the primary theoretical basis of this section, but the curriculum also stresses related theoretical concepts. Helping students transfer successful strategies of learning across academic programs by using techniques appropriate for different types of academic pursuits is the primary goal of this unit, so students learn techniques to memorize information at a surface level and then process information at deeper levels using elaborative techniques such as maps and networks.

The fourth part, self-change, presents a model of cognitive behavior modification and maintenance (Martin & Poland, 1980). Students design a project based on research and theory, present that research and design in a scholarly format, attempt the project for several weeks, and evaluate the results. During the research phase of the project, students learn to conduct research using different library database computer programs, and they become familiar with Internet resources. Operant and classical conditioning, reinforcement theory, positive self-talk, and collaborative partnerships are the focus of this section as students learn techniques to modify academic behaviors.

Throughout the course, faculty members use various techniques to evaluate students' progress. Papers, journals, projects, and tests comprise the normal structure. Tests, both traditional in-class objective and essay as well as take-home essay, comprise 60 to 75% of the grading criteria. Attendance and paper submission policies remain strict. Some students withdraw from the course because they are surprised by the academic rigor of the course, and they are unwilling to put forth the necessary effort. About 75% of students who complete the course earn a passing grade of a C or better. A perennial problem is the lack of suitable textbooks, although a few study skill books have begun to incorporate theory. Another problem is the lack of adequate graduate and in-service education possibilities. There are few graduate-level programs in developmental education. Most faculty members who teach learning framework courses come from related disciplines and have to dedicate themselves to independent study of the material to be taught.

Student Population

SWT is a regional comprehensive institution of higher education offering undergraduate and masters level instruction, as well as one doctoral program. Student enrollment is approximately 21,000. Several categories of undergraduate students register for EDP 1350. The first group includes students who are not experiencing academic problems but simply want to improve their grades or learning skills. Many of these students are first semester freshmen who hear about the course at summer orientation or are referred by students who have been in school for several semesters. Former students refer approximately 25% of students who take the course.

The second group are students who enter the university under regular admission procedures but experience academic difficulties at some point in their program. Typically, university officials refer students to the course as a condition of a special agreement they have made with students who have been suspended or are on academic appeal. Some of these students are required to take the course while others are strongly encouraged by their advisors, departmental chairs, or deans.

The third group is composed of a select group of conditionally admitted students who fail to meet regular admission requirements at the institution. These students are in the top three-quarters of their high school classes, but their test scores do not quite meet the general admission requirements. Students are granted conditional admission based on a consideration of high school courses taken and grades earned, the academic rigor of the senior year experience, specific rank in class, and English and mathematics scores on the Scholastic Aptitude Test (SAT) or American College Test (ACT). A select group of these students are required to take the course.

Marketing efforts for EDP 1350 have been extremely deliberate. The coordinator meets regularly with the academic deans or advisors, the admissions office staff, orientation advisors, athletic advisors, and other key university personnel. At the end of the fall term, the vice president for academic affairs sends a letter to selected freshmen who have been placed on probation. In that letter, he recommends that the student consider enrolling in EDP 1350 for the following term.

Instructors and Facilitators

A full-time tenured faculty member with a doctorate in developmental education coordinates the EDP 1350 program. Instructors are faculty members with degrees in educational psychology, developmental education, counseling, and reading. On occasion, part-time faculty members teach the course as well as advanced graduate students. New instructors receive close supervision and training from the coordinator and the more experienced instructors. Members of the faculty meet throughout the semester for continuous training and professional development. Faculty members participate in professional development through state and national organizations such as the National Association for Developmental Education (NADE), the College Reading and Learning Association (CRLA), and their local chapters.

Former students of EDP 1350 receive invitations to co-teach the class collaboratively with instructors. Although student facilitators, as they are called, may perform clerical duties, the focus of their work is to foster student learning. The role of the facilitator depends on the facilitator's talents and ambitions and the instructor's teaching style. Ideally, facilitators share the teaching activities. Facilitators ask questions and turn the class into a question and answer mode; give alternate explanations of the material (from a student's viewpoint); articulate a student's perspective on information; provide individual attention and feedback before, during, and after class; help supervise small group work and discussion; provide appropriate role models of active student learning; give encouragement; and change the climate of the classroom. EDP 1350 facilitators are unpaid volunteers (Hodges, Sellers, & White, 1994/95).

Research on Learning Framework Courses

Both SWT and UT-Austin have studied the effects of their learning framework courses on students' subsequent academic performance and retention. In a descriptive study conducted at UT-Austin, researchers (Weinstein, Roska, Hanson, & Van Mater Stone, 1997) found that freshmen who completed EDP 310 during the Fall 1990 and Spring 1991 semesters were retained for one year at higher rates than freshmen who did not take the course. The researchers also reported that students who completed the course earned higher first-year cumulative grade point averages (GPAs), failed fewer hours, and passed more courses. Freshmen with low SAT verbal and quantitative scores who enrolled in EDP 310 because they were predicted to be "at-

Table 1
T-test For Differences Between Freshmen and Freshmen Enrolled in EDP 1350, Fall 1991

	1st Semester Freshmen		Conditionally Admitted Freshmen	
	Freshman Enrolled in EDP 1350	All other Freshmen	Conditionally Admitted Freshmen Enrolled in EDP 1350	All Other Conditionally Admitted Freshmen
Mean Cumulative GPA 1st Semester	2.40* 87	2.09* 2914	2.18* 34	1.74* 879
Mean Cumulative GPA 2nd Semester	2.35* 85	2.20* 2382	2.16* 33	1.83* 698
Mean Cumulative GPA 3rd Semester	2.38 81	2.42 1694	2.24 31	2.10 469
One Year Retention (Students enrolled for Fall 1992)	93.10%* 81	58.13%* 1694	91.17%* 31	53.35%* 469
Mean SAT Verbal	389.00 70	403.88 2275	353.21 28	352.37 678
Mean SAT Quantitative	441.57 70	448.39 2275	402.86 28	389.84 678
Students Graduating in 6 Years	65.52%* 57	32.49%* 951	76.47%* 26	26.16%* 231

Note. Italicized numbers represent cell sizes.
Independent t-tests *$p < .05$.

risk" academically actually achieved higher GPAs and one-year retention rates than students not enrolled in the course.

A longitudinal study of EDP 1350 students at SWT produced several statistically significant results with regard to academic success and persistence. The study, conducted on first-semester freshmen enrolled in the course in 1991, revealed that both regularly admitted and conditionally admitted students who completed the course had significantly higher first-year GPAs, first-year retention rates, and six-year graduation rates than first-semester freshmen not enrolled in EDP 1350 (see Table 1).

The first two columns of data represent all entering freshmen, including those admitted conditionally. Although learning frameworks courses are not exclusively designed for at-risk populations, the researchers found that the conditionally admitted freshmen who completed

EDP 1350 had first-year retention rates and six-year graduation rates that compared favorably to those of the freshman population in general.

Current Status of Learning Framework Courses in Texas

In October 1999, after years of debate, the Texas Higher Education Coordinating Board (THECB) authorized formula funding of up to three semester credit hours for what were described as "Learning Framework" courses designed to improve students' understanding of the learning process and their ability to succeed in college. Four-year postsecondary institutions had offered such courses for many years, but prior to October 1999, all collegiate courses that focused primarily on the improvement of students' individual learning skills were classified as "developmental" and, consequently, were not eligible for formula funding. According to the THECB's recent decision, to receive formula funding learning framework courses must focus on (a) research and theory in the psychology of learning, cognition, and motivation; (b) factors that impact learning; and (c) application of learning strategies (Texas Higher Education Coordinating Board, 1999). SWT and UT-Austin are the two institutions currently offering a course that meets the new criteria. Faculty and administrators from both institutions were instrumental in shaping the new statewide policy.

Implications

Learning framework courses merit funding and traditional academic status; these courses are developmental in nature, not remedial, and also have a strong academic content based in cognitive psychology research and theory. Research data support that learning framework courses aid retention, success, and graduation of undergraduate students. Much needs to be done to disseminate this information to the various constituencies of higher education: students, faculty, staff, administrators, trustees, legislators, and publishers. As developmental educators continue to investigate and promote learning framework courses, more students will succeed academically.

References

Bandura, A. (1993). Perceived self-efficacy in cognitive development and functioning. *Educational Psychologist, 28*, 177-148.

Boylan, H.R. (1999). Exploring alternatives to remediation. *Journal of Developmental Education, 22*(3), 2-4, 6, 8, 10.

Branden, N. (1994). *The six pillars of self-esteem*. New York: Bantam.

Briggs, K.C., & Myers, I.B. (1998). *Myers-Briggs Type Indicator*. Palo Alto, CA: Consulting Psychologists.

Cole R.P., Babcock, C., Goetz, E.T., & Weinstein, C.E. (1997, October). *An in-depth look at academic success courses*. Paper presented at the meeting of the College Reading and Learning Association, Sacramento, CA.

Gagné, E.D., Yekovich, C.W., & Yekovich, F.R. (1993). *Cognitive psychology of school learning* (2nd ed.). New York: Harper Collins.

Gardner, H. (1993). *Multiple intelligences: The theory in practice*. New York: Harper Collins.

Hodges, R.B., Sellers, D.E., & White, W.G. (1994-95). Peer teaching: The use of facilitators in college classes. *Journal of College Reading and Learning, 26*(2), 23-29.

Kolb, D.A. (1999). *Learning Style Inventory* (Version 3). Boston: Hay/McBer.

Martin, R.A., & Poland, E.Y. (1980). *Learning to change*. New York: McGraw-Hill.

Maslow, A.H. (1970). *Motivation and personality* (2nd ed.). New York: Harper & Row.

Maxwell, M. (1997). *Improving student learning skills*. Clearwater, FL: H & H.

Peck, M.S. (1978). *The road less traveled*. New York: Simon & Schuster.

Perry, W.G., Jr. (1968). *Forms of intellectual and ethical development in the college years*. New York: Holt, Rinehart and Winston.

Pintrich, P. (1995). Understanding self-regulated learning. In P. Pintrich (Ed.), *Understanding self-regulated learning* (pp. 3-12). San Francisco: Jossy-Bass.

Pintrich, P.R., McKeachie, W.J., & Lin, Y. (1987). Teaching a course in learning to learn. *Teaching of Phychology, 14*(2), 81-85.

Stahl, N.A., Hynd, C.R., & Henk, W.A. (1986). Avenues for chronicling and researching the history of college reading and study skills instruction. *Journal of Reading, 29*, 334-341.

Texas Higher Education Coordinating Board (1999). Consideration of board policy on funding of courses designed to improve students' understanding of the learning process and their ability to succeed in college. *Texas Higher Education Coordinating Board Quarterly Meeting October, 28, 1999* (Agenda Item 5G). Austin, TX: Texas Higher Education Coordinating Board.

Weiner. B. (1986). *An attribution theory of motivation and emotion*. New York: Academic Press.

Weinstein, C.E. (1994). Strategic learning/strategic teaching: Flip sides of a coin. In P.R. Pintrich, D.R. Brown, & C.E. Weinstein (Eds.) *Student motivation, cognition, and learning* (pp. 257-273). Hillsdale, NJ: Lawrence Erlbaum.

Weinstein, C.E., Dierking, D., Husman, J., Roska, L., & Powdrill, L. (1998). The impact of a course in strategic learning on the long-term retention of college students. In J.L. Higbee & P.L. Dwinnel (Eds.), *Developmental education: Preparing successful college students* (pp. 85-96). Columbia, SC: National Resource Center for The First-Year Experience and Students in Transition.

Weinstein, C.E., Palmer, D.R., & Schulte, A.C. (1987). *Learning and study strategy inventory*. Clearwater, FL: H & H.

Weinstein, C.E., Roska, L.A., Hanson, G.R., & Van Mater Stone, G. (1997, March). *EDP 310: A course in strategic learning*. Paper presented Courses for Academic Success Symposium at the Annual Meeting of the American Educational Research Association, Chicago, IL.

When ESL is Developmental:
A Model Program for the Freshman Year

Robin Murie & Renata Thomson
University of Minnesota

Abstract

Growing numbers of language-minority high school graduates find themselves placed into English as a Second Language (ESL) courses at the college level. The Commanding English Program (CE) at the University of Minnesota is designed to serve immigrant and refugee students, a population with distinct academic needs including language support, content that engages critical thinking and allows novice writers to practice and gain confidence, and connection to other students, advisors, and mentors on campus. Above all, students need the education and academic credits of the freshman year. The program, rooted in principles of developmental education, offers a supported freshman year curriculum for these language-minority students.

Mohamed's first six years of schooling took place in his native Somalia, where he learned in Arabic in Quranic school, and in Somali for nonreligious schooling. Civil war came suddenly, forcing him to flee to Kenya, where it became prudent to learn Swahili to help his two brothers run a makeshift store in a refugee camp. Attending junior high was out of the question. Four years later, he found himself in a large urban high school in Minneapolis, trying to make up for lost time in his education. He was now taking a combination of bilingual

For additional information contact: Robin Murie • General College • University of Minnesota • 233 Appleby Hall • 128 Pleasant Street SE • Minneapolis, MN 55455 • e-mail: rmurie@umn.edu

Somali and English classes, learning to negotiate the cafeteria in his fourth language, riding a bus across town for extra tutoring in fractions and decimals so that he could survive in pre-algebra, and spending hours every night trying to read his textbooks. As a university freshman, Mohamed needs more than English as a Second Language (ESL) courses. He needs academic support through the content of the freshman year. To be successful at the university, he needs to meet the challenge of reading 30 pages of literature per night, to acquire the strategies for studying biology and managing the load of medical terminology and systems, and to gain practice with writing and revising research-based academic papers.

Trinh, in contrast, had close to 14 years of formal education before coming to the university. She graduated from a rigorous high school in Vietnam, but was denied access to higher education there for political reasons. Her family chose to join relatives in the U.S., in part for the educational opportunities here. Trinh repeated the last two years of high school in Minnesota in order to prepare for college courses in English. She, too, benefits from the support of tutorials, specially designed sections of writing and speech, and small class size to develop confidence and fluency in academic English.

Mohammed and Trinh belong to a growing number of refugee and immigrant students in the U.S. In the Minneapolis school district alone, two of the large urban high schools report that one third of their students receive ESL services. As permanent residents and graduates of U.S. high schools, these students are expected to face the same academic challenges as the mainstream college population. But in addition to the new level of literacy required for all students to thrive as college freshmen (Johns, 1992), they must acquire "insider knowledge of the rhetorical communities [they] wish to enter" (Soter, 1992). This insider knowledge is inevitably less accessible to language minority students than to native English speakers because it is implicit and culturally based (Curie, 1993). Labeled by some as "Generation 1.5" (Rumbaut & Ima, 1988, cited by Harklau, Losey, & Siegel, 1999), or the "transitional generation" (Luoma, Pfankuch, & Reardon, 1991), language minority students must negotiate between cultures. At times they may see their home culture as a deficit to be overcome in order to succeed (Lu, 1992). At other times they may experience alienation from the university because they do not see their experiences or cultures being represented there or because they are perceived by themselves and others as outsiders. Such students face additional struggles not faced by majority students (Collins, 1999). Their literacy needs extend beyond simple language instruction.

Traditional ESL programs work from a linguistic base, offering students ways to learn the English language through courses in reading, writing, listening, and grammar. At the University of Minnesota, for example, the Minnesota English Center offers an intensive English program (IEP) for international students. These students take a combination of regular academic courses and noncredit ESL classes until their Test of English as a Foreign Language (TOEFL) scores reach the proficiency level required by the university.

Although this linguistic focus is appropriate for the well-educated international student who primarily needs some practice with English before resuming a full academic load, it does not address the needs of the high school graduate language-minority student who may be underprepared for university study. The Commanding English (CE) program, therefore, offers a different model for delivering academic ESL. The program was designed to address the needs of immigrant and refugee students in terms of both language and academic content. English-enriched courses are offered in an integrated full year program, providing a rigorous yet supported freshman curriculum.

The support offered by CE is based on a number of assumptions about language learning and developmental education. It combines features of proven models in developmental programs, such as learning communities, Supplemental Instruction, peer tutorials, and small class size. Advising incorporates career and transfer planning, critical to any student but particularly to first-generation college students whose families may not have established career paths in the U.S. Now in its 21st year, CE, a program of the University of Minnesota's General College (GC), serves as an entry point to the university for 50 to 75 language-minority students annually. Placement into the program is determined by the admissions office and based on American College Testing (ACT) and Michigan English Language Assessment Battery (MELAB) or Test of English as a Foreign Language (TOEFL) scores for students who have been in English-speaking schools for fewer than eight years.

Commanding English Program

Students enroll in Commanding English for an entire year, two semesters of full-time coursework. Classes are offered in "sets" so that the same cohort of 15 to 17 students can form a

Figure 1. Curriculum in the Commanding English Program

Fall Semester

- Anthropology, General Arts, Sociology (choose one) , 4-5 credits
- Reading Adjunct (uses the text of the above course), 2 credits
- Basic Writing I (CE Section), 3 credits
- Writing (Grammar) Workshop, 2 credits
- Speech (CE Section), 3 credits

Spring Semester

- Biology, Anthropology, Sociology (choose one), 4-5 credits
- Reading Adjunct to above course (CE), 2 credits
- Basic Writing II (CE Section), 3 credits
- Literature of the American Immigrant Experience, 3 credits

learning community, taking three to four courses together in a semester. A specially trained advisor meets regularly with students to discuss registration and transfer plans, and peer tutors from the Writing Center attend the writing classes to assist students on a daily basis. A typical curriculum for a semester includes 13 to 15 credits (see Figure 1).

Students who are planning a major in the Institute of Technology often begin math coursework in the spring semester. Students may also enroll in physical education, music, or a career-planning seminar. Students may choose to retake the MELAB or TOEFL if they wish to exit the program after the first semester. There is no mandatory exit testing, however.

Assumptions Behind the Approach

The Commanding English Program is informed by a number of assumptions about language learning and developmental education.

Language Learning Takes Time

Half of the students in CE report knowing three or more languages well. These are not poor language learners working from a deficit, but they are often judged as such because the education system fails to acknowledge that language acquisition takes time. As Hakuta (2000) notes, "policies that assume rapid acquisition of English . . . are wildly unrealistic" (p. 13). Cummins' influential study (1981) makes a distinction between conversational language and the more cognitively demanding language needed for academic work. Basic interpersonal communications skills (BICS) tend to be used in context-rich situations that are not necessarily cognitively demanding. BICS include basic conversational abilities that are often acquired most effectively via immersion in the target language. Cognitive academic language proficiency (CALP) includes skills that tend to be used in context-reduced and cognitively demanding situations, such as doing academic work at the college level. BICS and CALP typically develop at different rates. As might be expected, conversational skills can be mastered in a few years. It takes four to six years, or longer, to build academic language (Cummins 1981).

The variables that affect language acquisition and the amount of time it requires include, but are not limited to, the level of literacy reached in the home language, and the age of an individual when first exposed to the target language. Collier and Thomas (1997) have been conducting research since 1985 on how long English acquisition takes for immigrant children in Canada. They found that students who arrived between ages eight and eleven, who had received at least two to five years of schooling taught through their primary language in their home country, took only five to seven years to acquire CALP. "Those who arrived before age eight . . . [with] little or no formal schooling in their first language . . . required seven to ten years or more" (p. 33). These variables affect the population of the Commanding English Program: some students have arrived even more recently in the U.S. than those discussed by Collier and Thomas, and with even less formal schooling in the home language. The program recognizes the need for time and does not try to "fix their English" or to teach academic skills in a few classes, but rather offers a full year of supported coursework. The goal is to facilitate these students' development as college-level readers and writers of English. The research of Collier and Thomas indicates that with adequate time allowed, this goal is realistic: "Allowed to continue in college . . . their pattern during high school of making more gains than the native-English speaker with each year of schooling would predict that they would close the gap sometime during their undergraduate schooling" (pp. 33-34).

Students Need the Education and Credit of the Freshman Year

Students who have entered U.S. schools from other countries may well be facing some educational gaps, either because of the time it takes to catch up in a new language or because of missed schooling due to the turmoil of the refugee process. The perception that ESL students are not ready for college coursework "often implies instruction that focuses on grammar, decontextualized language skills and surface features of language" (Zamel, 1998). However, as Zamel adds, "learning is responsive to situations in which students are invited to participate in the construction of meaning and knowledge" (p. 260). In other words, it is not enough to address language needs in isolation from other kinds of learning, and in fact, it is a richer model of language acquisition when the learner is attending to meaning, not language (Brinton, Snow, & Wesche, 1989). Students also need the content of the social sciences, sciences, humanities, and math, (Adamson, 1993; Harklau et al., 1999; Zamel, 1998). Collier and Thomas (1997) stress that demands for English-language-only classes in public schools are "simplistic" because when we teach only the English language we are literally slowing down a child's cognitive and academic growth, and that child "may never catch up to the constantly advancing native-English speaker" (p. 41). At the college level, when many language-minority students continue this process of catching up, what they need remains the same: "multiple opportunities to use language and write-to-learn . . . classroom exchanges and assignments that promote the acquisition of unfamiliar language, concepts and approaches to inquiry" (Zamel, p. 261).

The issue of credit-bearing coursework is a controversial one. ESL coursework is often defined as basic or remedial, and therefore not worthy of college credit. One can argue that the "acquisition of a new language requires as much or more effort than is required of typical college level courses" (Van Meter, 1990, p. 2). For refugee and immigrant students, it is important that courses be for credit: "Immigrants often attend college on the thinnest of financial margins and financial aid is a key factor in their persistence (or attrition) in degree programs" (Harklau et al., 1999, p. 7). Credit increases immigrant students' motivation both to sign up for a class in the first place, and to work towards a high grade point average (GPA) they perceive as necessary to their future success in the U.S. In CE classes it is also appropriate that students receive credit because they are expected to hone English language skills within core courses and adjunct courses that also require rigorous work in the content areas themselves.

Students Benefit from Individual Attention

Small class size, the availability of peer tutors and writing centers, specialized advising, and career and transfer planning are important to all students. To those who are first generation immigrants, and who may feel marginalized by cultural differences, individual attention becomes even more important. In the 1999 NADE monograph, Burrell and Kim describe some of the difficulties experienced by international students due to "differences in communication patterns and the stresses involved in trying new ones," (p. 87) and how these cultural adjustments may be even more difficult to make when students are also concerned about making language errors in group situations. In their discussion of the rationale for including international students within the developmental education service population, Burrell and Kim imply that it is inappropriate to view language minority students simply as needing help with basic skills. Rather, the goal should be to enhance the learning process through sensitivity to the multiple needs of students. Small class size and the formation of learning communities can help set an inclusive atmosphere for students who might not otherwise have a voice as freshmen at a large university. Figure 2 summarizes the support CE provides for language-minority students in their first year of college.

Figure 2. Summary of support for language-minority freshmen

Types of support language-minority students need in their first year of college:

- Time to develop as a student
- Language support: ways to build academic vocabulary and manage large reading loads, and grammar review that is connected to writing
- Strategies for drafting and revising, and for proofreading and editing
- Development of study skills and test taking strategies
- Practice with academic voice, with the "experience of remembering others' work, referencing it, pulling it in at just the right place in one's own emerging text, transforming it to serve one's own ends, and giving it space without privileging it over one's own words" (Blanton, 1999, p. 137)
- Time and support and content that engages critical thinking and allows novice writers to practice and gain confidence
- Sense of belonging to a cohort on campus, being connected to other students, advisors and mentors on campus
- Above all, students need the education and credits of the freshman year

Building a Curriculum

Students can be supported through college courses in a variety of ways:

1. Tutors can be brought into classes.

2. The curriculum can offer separate parallel sections of courses to increase language-minority students' comfort level in class and to allow some modification of course content to address specific needs.

3. Supplemental Instruction, tutorials, and reading adjunct courses can be provided.

4. By registering for several courses together, students can form learning communities that offer both social and academic support.

The Commanding English curriculum uses all of these: modified parallel sections, tutors, supplemental reading courses, and the building of learning communities. What follows is a description of some of the courses in the Commanding English program and how support is built into the curriculum. This is not offered as a definitive list but rather as an example of how some typical freshman courses can be supported or modified to better accommodate the needs of second-language students.

Basic Writing

"Anecdotal evidence suggests that developmental writing courses may become de facto ESL writing courses, and writing centers are often overrun with nonnative language writers who have no other means of language support" (Harklau et al., 1999, p. 6). The CE program offers its own sections of Basic Writing in order to incorporate language support into the course, and it actively collaborates with the General College Writing Center to extend this support.

All students benefit from a writing course that incorporates extensive reading, analysis, writing, and revising to help novice writers develop greater proficiency with source-based writing, whether that writing is in the first or the second-language. The writing process itself is not different in second language writing, but the writer may feel more constrained and less sure of linguistic and rhetorical conventions (Silva, 1993). A second-language writer may need modification in the choice of readings, the length of the readings, the amount of in-class writing, and the attention given to linguistic features of writing. Second-language writing teachers need to "devote more time and attention across the board to strategies, rhetorical and linguistic concerns" (Silva, p. 670).

In the parallel Commanding English sections of basic writing, the topics in the course are similar to the other sections offered in the college; the same number of major papers are required, and course activities are much the same: students read, draft, revise, and discuss their writing with each other. This process is easier for language-minority students in classes designed specifically for them because students are less likely to be silenced by the social distance that can be created by the presence of native speakers (Hodne, 1997). There is also a question of comfort level in a class that focuses on one's ability to communicate effectively in English. The Commanding English sections differ from regular sections of writing in that the readings tend to be shorter and more carefully selected for accessibility. Instead of a book-length work, a reading packet of eight to ten shorter excerpts is typically used. Also, more class time is spent discussing the readings; there is less in-class timed writing, and peer tutors work with students in the CE writing courses. The other significant difference is the number of drafts. Students write three drafts, the first for content, the second for language attention, and the third for a grade.

Speech

Similar to Basic Writing, Commanding English offers parallel sections of a freshman public speaking course, again following the same course content and goals, but providing a less intimidating environment for giving oral presentations, in which classmates will not discount accented speech. The focus of this course is on training students to become effective communicators through the preparation and presentation of individual speeches and a group debate. For students with accented speech, compensation strategies, such as using visual support, repetition, comprehension checks, and slowing down, are also emphasized. Students critique videotapes of their presentations, allowing them to become familiar with their own communication style.

Grammar

Grammar instruction at this level seems to be most effective when it is tied to a student's own writing and editing strategies. Some formal presentation of grammar material may be useful, especially for students who did not have much explicit language instruction as they learned English. This helps students to build editing tools to assist them as they check over their writing. Connecting grammar to writing can be done through tutorials, in a writing lab, through a drafting process that specifically tends to linguistic features, or through a grammar course that has an editing focus (Murie, 1997). In the Commanding English program a grammar workshop is connected with the first semester basic writing course. In this workshop course, students focus on strategies for editing their own writing for language concerns. There are three components to the workshop: in-class presentation and study of particular grammar areas; tutorials where students meet individually with the peer tutor from their writing class to check their own writing for the particular grammar topic of the week; and small-group meetings with the instructor to analyze comments and corrections made on the papers students write in the basic writing course. This gives students a forum for asking questions about the grammar editing comments written on their papers and for analyzing their own language use as a way of becoming more conscious of the proofreading and editing issues in their writing.

Adjunct Reading Courses

Undergraduates must fulfill distribution requirements in the social sciences, humanities, and science. These survey courses offer numerous challenges for second-language students, including the difficult reading and vocabulary load of the textbooks, the assumed background knowledge in a course such as sociology or history, the intricacies of how a multiple choice test is worded, the fast pace of a professor's lecture, and the discomfort of class participation.

A reading adjunct course, building on models of Supplemental Instruction, gives students support for the academic content while, at the same time, helps students build reading skills. The adjunct course is taught by the ESL instructor using the reading material from the survey course, thus allowing students to build reading skills within the context of content areas. Reading biology is different from reading sociology: the former requires considerable skills in learning the details and vocabulary of science systems. In sociology, students need to learn to read more generally and more critically. What is the bias in a given article? How do various readings relate to the topic of sociology? In biology, much of the vocabulary work is with roots, prefixes, and suffixes; in sociology, more work is done with building contexts for words, for guessing at meaning.

In all the adjunct courses, in addition to reading skills and vocabulary development, students are also getting academic support to help them navigate the content course. There is time to ask questions about lecture content, to go over the material again, providing the key repetition needed for language acquisition. Students are also getting strategic information: how to use a professor's office hours; how to take multiple choice exams; and how to manage time and take effective lecture and reading notes.

Sociology

Sociology is a popular choice among students. The course "People and Problems" covers social problems of the U.S. such as racism, poverty, gender, and health care. A student from Vietnam commented last year that this open discussion of problems gives him a new understanding of freedom in the U.S. because people can openly discuss the social problems of the country. The reading adjunct connected to this course focuses on point of view, and on reading skills themselves such as previewing material, understanding the context for key vocabulary, reading for the main ideas, taking notes on reading passages, and relating issues across readings.

Biology

This course focuses on human anatomy and physiology, a common prerequisite for students who are interested in careers in the health sciences. The course itself is quite rigorous with difficult exams, an intense vocabulary load of learning the major systems of the human body, and learning basic dissection laboratory techniques. The reading adjunct paired with this course focuses on how to read a dense science text, how to prepare for multiple choice exams, strategies for memorizing the parts of the ten major systems and their physiological processes, and extensive vocabulary work with affixes and stems. The biology professor often conducts review sessions with the students during the adjunct class at the invitation of the instructor as anatomy and physiology is typically not the expertise of the reading instructor.

Cultural Anthropology

In this course the Commanding English students often hold an advantage over their monolingual, mono-cultural classmates. Anthropology professors see the benefit to having students with a variety of cultural backgrounds in their course. The Sudanese student who challenges the textbook's representation of the Nuwer tribe is a resource in the course that more than compensates for whatever limitations the student might have with written English or accented speech. The CE reading adjunct teacher in this course assists students with the reading load, assigns group discussions of chapter material, and works with students on anticipating test questions, reviewing lecture notes, building an individualized academic vocabulary base, and discussing strategies for taking essay exams.

The professors who agree to have Commanding English students linked with their courses are given extra training in ways to accommodate for language development. These techniques are good pedagogy for any student: ways to lecture so that oral instructions and terminology are also provided in written form; allowing for extra time on in-class writing; preparing students for class discussion by starting with written or small-group discussion of the topic to give students an opportunity to formulate a response; and providing reading guides. One sociology professor allowed students in his class to take exams either in essay or multiple-choice format. CE students typically did better on the essays, without the linguistic maze that a multiple-choice exam can present. One of the biology professors frequently visited the reading class to answer questions and make contact with the students. Another sociology professor constructed group discussion of the readings in ways that allowed her students opportunities to analyze and ask questions in small groups before the all-class discussion. The reading adjunct teacher also becomes a resource for the professor who may have questions about appropriate accommodations or student progress in the course.

Literature

Another way to support a curriculum is to design a content course specifically for that curriculum. At the University of Minnesota's General College, GC 1364 "Literature of the American Immigrant Experience," is a three-credit literature course offered through Commanding English, with seats open on a space-available basis to other students at the university. The course explores immigration history and common themes through literature written by and about immigrants. The reading load includes four novels. A typical sequence might include *Thousand Pieces of Gold* by Ruthanne Lum McCunn (1981); *Bread Givers*, by Anzia Yezierska (1925); *No No Boy* by John Okada (1957); *House on Mango Street* by Sandra Cisneros (1984); historical documents; and the text *A Different Mirror* by R. Takaki (1993). Writing is source based, using evidence from different novels and historical documents to discuss themes across literature and to examine ways in which literature illuminates and interprets history.

Although the reading load of 25 to 30 pages a night is heavy for some, students have the intellectual and experiential background for the course. Novels are selected deliberately with an eye to the level of vocabulary and idiom. A developmental approach is taken with the essays written about each novel: students are given advice on how to write the essay; sample essays are given out and analyzed, and the first two essays are written in a drafted process, with teacher feedback. Students receive guidance about how to organize an essay with a clear focus and how to integrate quoted material into the discussion. Toward the end of the semester, students are expected to be able to do this on their own, and the teacher's assistance shifts to research strategies for the final project.

Can students manage a college literature course while they are still at the ESL level? Yes, if the course selects texts carefully, builds developmental components into the assignments, and demands that students meet the expectations. A further benefit comes from students finding their own stories in the literature. In a 1999 study of participants in Commanding English literature courses, students "felt that not only did they learn new academic skills, but also that their motivation to learn and succeed was positively impacted by the relevancy of the curriculum to their experiences" (Collins, 1999, p. 11).

Table 1.
Number of CE students who have graduated or are still enrolled at the University

Year	Number of Students	Percentages of CE students who have graduated or are still enrolled at the University each year (Y1, Y2, etc.)				
		Y1	Y2	Y3	Y4	Y5
1989	53	92	77	62	60	58
1990	51	88	75	61	51	41
1991	51	86	73	65	55	51
1992	50	96	88	76	66	60
1993	54	96	89	80	72	63
1994	62	94	89	81	71	52
1995	65	98	91	80	66	
1996	48	94	85	73		
1997	50	94	82			

Does the Program Work?

Twenty years of history shows that the Commanding English program succeeds in meeting its goals. Retention rates through the first year are high, as one might predict in a program built on learning communities with small class size, personalized advising, tutorial support, and a curriculum designed for second-language learners. In the past 11 years, first-year retention rates have ranged from a low of 86% to a high of 98%. By the end of the sophomore year, retention figures are 73% to 91%, a rate that is significantly higher than for other students in the General

College. In the third year 61% to 81% of the students have successfully transferred to one of the degree-granting colleges at the University of Minnesota and are in good standing (see Table 1). In the words of the Office of Research and Evaluation (ORE) report: "CE students are retained at a higher rate than are non-CE GC students, and they show much higher rates of transfer" (Hatfield, 2000).

Given the length of time it takes some students to complete degree programs, graduation rates are more difficult to measure. In a Spring 2000 retention report, graduation rates for Commanding English students 1991 to 1994 who transferred into one of the degree-granting colleges at the University ranged between 29% and 57%. These percentages do not take into account students who transferred to another university or college to complete a professional degree. What happens to the nongraduates? We have not done a formal study to look at the reasons for leaving the University. Anecdotally we know of students who needed to return to full-time employment to support family, who were denied access to professional schools (e.g. nursing, pharmacy) at the university and so transferred to other colleges to complete their degree, who have switched majors and have not graduated within five years, whose family circumstances interfered, and some who have lacked the academic preparation or motivation to thrive at the university.

Summary

The goal of the Commanding English program is to offer high-level academic English in a credit-bearing curriculum that provides enough support for students through their freshman year. It is a model of instruction that both respects a student's need to progress academically and fosters literacy growth over time. At the end of the year students have completed freshman writing, speech, literature, a social science, and a humanities or science requirement; they have written over 15 papers and have learned how to research, revise, and use tutors in the writing center as a resource. They have presented research material both orally and in writing, have had extensive experience working collaboratively with other students, reading chapters of material, drafting and revising papers. Is the English error free? In many cases, no. But the student is well on the way to being a sophomore, with a stronger voice and experience with the rigors of college coursework.

References

Adamson, H.D. (1993). *Academic competence: Theory and classroom practice: Preparing ESL students for content courses*. White Plains, NY: Longman.

Blanton, L.L. (1999). Classroom instruction and language minority students: On teaching to "smarter" readers and writers. In L. Harklau, K.M. Losey, & M. Siegal (Eds.), *Generation 1.5 meets college composition: Issues in the teaching of writing to U.S. educated learners of ESL* (pp. 119-142). Mahwah, NJ: Lawrence Erlbaum Associates.

Brinton, D.M., & Snow, M.B. (1989). *Content-based second language instruction*. Boston: Heinle & Heinle.

Burrell, K.I., & Kim. D.J. (1998). International students and academic assistance: Meeting the needs of another college population. In P.L. Dwinell & J.L. Higbee (Eds.), Developmental education: Meeting diverse student needs (pp. 81-96). Morrow, GA: National Association for Developmental Education.

Cisneros, S. (1984). *House on Mango Street*. New York: Vintage Books.

Collier, V., & Thomas, W. (1997). *Our findings: The "how long" research* [Online]. Available: ncbe.gwu.edu/ncbpubs/resource/effectiveness/Thomas-Collier 97.pdf.

Collins, M. (1999). The multicultural classroom: Immigrants reading the literature of the American immigrant experience. Unpublished masters thesis, University of Minnesota.

Cummins, J. (1981). Age on arrival and immigrant second language learning in Canada: A reassessment. *Applied Linguistics, 2*, 131-149.

Curie, P. (1993, May). Entering a disciplinary community: Conceptual activities required to write for one university course. *Journal of Second Language Writing, 2* (2), 101-117.

Hakuta, K. (2000). *Improving education for all children: Meeting the needs of language minority children* [Online]. Available: http://www.stanford.edu/~hakuta/Aspen.html

Harklau, L, Losey, K.M. & Siegal, M. (1999). Linguistically diverse students and college writing: What is equitable and appropriate? In L. Harklau, K.M. Losey, & M. Siegal (Eds.), *Generation 1.5 meets college composition: Issues in the teaching of writing to U.S. educated learners of ESL* (pp. 1-14). Mahwah, NJ: Lawrence Erlbaum Associates.

Hatfield, J. (2000). *Commanding English Tracking Study*, Office of Research and Evaluation, General College, University of Minnesota.

Hodne, B.D. (1997). Please speak up: Asian immigrant students in American college classrooms. In D.L. Sigsbee, B.W. Speck, & B. Maylath (Eds.), *Approaches to teaching non-native English speakers across the curriculum*. New Directions in Teaching and Learning, No. 70 (pp. 85-92). San Francisco: Jossey-Bass.

Johns, A.M. (1992). Toward developing a cultural repertoire: A case study of a Lao college freshman. In D.E. Murray (Ed.), *Diversity as resource: Redefining cultural literacy*. Alexandria, VA: Teachers of English to Speakers of Other Languages (TESOL).

Lu, M. (1992). Conflict and struggle: The enemies or preconditions of basic writing. *College English, 54*, (8).

Luoma, A., Pfankuch, J., & Reardon, M. (1991). The transitional generation: Growing up in two worlds. *International Student*, 14-17.

McCunn, R.L. (1981). *Thousand pieces of gold*. Boston: Beacon.

Murie, R. (1997). Building editing skills: Putting students at the center of the editing process. In D.L. Sigsbee, B.W. Speck, & B. Maylath (Eds.), *Approaches to teaching non-native English speakers across the curriculum*. New Directions in Teaching and Learning, No. 70 (pp. 85-92). San Francisco: Jossey-Bass.

Okada, J. (1957). *No no boy*. Seattle: University of Washington.

Rumbaut, R.G., & Ima, K. (1988). The adaptation of Southeast Asian refugee youth: A comparative study. (Final report to the Office of Resettlement). San Diego, CA: San Diego State University. (ERIC Document Reproduction Service No. ED 299372)

Silva, T. (1993). Towards an understanding of the distinct nature of L2 writing: The ESL research and its implications. *TESOL Quarterly, 27*, 657-677.

Soter, A. (1992) Whose shared assumptions? Making the implicit explicit. In D. Murray (Ed.), *Diversity as resource: Redefining cultural literacy* (pp. 30-55). Alexandria, VA: Teachers of English to Speakers of Other Languages (TESOL).

Takaki, R. (1993) *A different mirror: A history of multicultural America*. Boston: Little, Brown.

Van Meter, J. (1990.) Academic credit for ESL classes. *Research in Development Education, 8,* (1).

Yezierska, A. (1925). *Bread givers*. New York: Pearsea.

Zamel, V. (1998). Strangers in academia: The experiences of faculty and ESL students across the curriculum. In V. Zamel & R. Spack (Eds.), *Negotiating academic literacies* (pp. 249-263). Mahwah, NJ: Lawrence Erlbaum Associates.

Narrative Therapy
and College Basic Writers

Mary P. Deming
Georgia State University

Abstract

This chapter begins with a description of a new movement in psychotherapy, narrative therapy. Narrative therapy is based on the theory of social construction that asserts that realities are created through language and are organized and maintained through narratives . Some of the tools of narrative therapy are useful with at-risk college students, in particular college basic writers, to assist them in deconstructing myths about their academic lives in order to replace stories of academic failures with stories of academic success.

One day as I was packing up my books to leave after a scheduled session of conferences with my writing students, one of my young male students appeared, late for his scheduled appointment. He immediately pulled up a desk and sat down right in front of me. Responding to my seemingly innocuous prompt, "How's it going?" he hung down his head and let loose a torrent of sorrows, recalling his failed attempt as an athlete and as a student at a small Midwestern college and his role in the unplanned pregnancy of a young local woman. Losing his scholarship, he returned to his home city where life did not improve as he quickly married another woman. He described this difficult marriage, his feelings of inadequacy in the university, and his experiences with a violent, alcoholic family member. Finally, he stopped

For additional information contact: Mary P. Deming • Georgia State University • Department of Middle/Secondary Education and Instructional Technology • University Plaza • Atlanta, GA 30303-3083 • e-mail: mstmpd@langate.gsu.edu talking, shook his head repeatedly, and said in despair, "I am so unhappy; I am so unhappy." We sat in silence for a long while as I was stunned by the sadness of his story, and he was exhausted from the telling of it. Prudently, I decided that this was not the appropriate time to discuss his writing problems.

Not all of my students suffer such a degree of sorrow as this young man, and many educators would argue that it is not the domain of college basic writing instructors to intervene in this personal aspect of students' lives. Rather, some might say, "Leave it to the counselors." But, in reality, many students come to college with stories detailing various experiences of sadness and suffering, emanating from both their personal and academic lives, and these stressful situations still influence their lives and may negatively affect their academic success in varying degrees. In addition, in less extreme cases, many of our students come to college with a deep sense of personal academic failure, bringing with them stories describing horrors from their past school lives. In particular, many at-risk college students view themselves as their academic deficiencies. They have been indoctrinated to follow the deficit model of education, seeing themselves solely as poor Scholastic Aptitude Test (SAT) scores, or low grade-point averages GPAs), or poor readers, writers, and students. As a result, few students when placed in pre-college level classes really view college as a fresh start. Obviously, the reasons for lack of student success and perseverance in college are complicated and intertwined. The most obvious reason for failure or for flight, of course, is academic, but some retention experts believe that noncognitive reasons, or affective variables, are equally influential in determining student success (Bean & Metzner, 1985; Broughton, 1986; Tinto, 1993). For some students with severe personal tragedies, instructor sensitivity and referrals to counselors or other experts may be all that we can offer, but for others, those who come with negative academic baggage from the past, we can provide opportunities to help them to begin to overcome their troubling academic histories.

Perhaps an interdisciplinary approach to this academic problem should be considered. In the field of psychology today, many therapists are using narratives to help their clients to restory their lives, replacing negative stories with new stories offering positive identities. Perchance educators should borrow back some of the tools from psychology, namely those from narrative therapy, to help basic writing students restory their academic lives.

The Tenets of Narrative Therapy

Narrative therapy, according to therapist Bill O'Hanlon (1994), ". . . represents a fundamentally new direction in the therapeutic world, a movement that might be called psychotherapy's Third Wave" (p. 22). According to O'Hanlon, the first wave of psychotherapy was "pathology-focused and dominated by psychodynamic theories and biological psychiatry . . . it focused so heavily on pathology that it skewed our view of human nature" (p. 22). With the second wave of psychology, people's problems "resided in small-scale systems; solutions still rested with therapists . . ." (p. 22). However, a shift occurred in the 1980s with the onset of competence-based therapies when many therapists started to believe that focusing on problems often blocks resources and solutions residing within clients. Many therapists began no longer to see themselves as the problem-solvers, but instead believed solutions are lived within clients.

Freedman and Combs (1996) assert that narrative therapy has its roots in a new set of metaphors: narrative and social construction. They believe that therapists using the techniques of narrative therapy are supported by the ideas associated with the social constructivist view of the world. These ideas include the following:

1. Realities are socially constructed.

2. Realities are constituted through language.

3. Realities are organized and maintained through narrative.

4. There are no essential truths. (p. 22)

Realities are socially constructed through social interaction through time. "In other words, people construct their realities as they live them" (Freedman and Combs, 1996, p. 23). Berger and Luckmann (1966) delineate the three processes involved in social construction: typification, institutionalization, and legitimation. They state that these three processes are important for a social group to construct and maintain its view of reality. Reification, which describes the total process, is defined by Berger and Luckmann (1966) as:

the apprehension of the products of human activity *as if* they were something else than human products—such as facts of nature, results of cosmic laws, or manifestations of divine will. Reification implies that man [sic] is capable of forgetting his ownership of the human world. (p. 89)

Language is the tool people use to construct their view of the world, for people use language to share their realities. Anderson and Goolishian (1988) write "Language does not mirror nature; language creates the natures we know" (p. 378). So too, language not only creates narrative, but it also keeps it alive as people share their stories. Bruner (1991) writes that ". . . we organize our experience and our memory of human happenings mainly in the form of narratives—stories, excuses, myths, reasons for doing and not doing, and so on" (p. 4). Finally, in the social construction view, many scholars believe there is no objective reality, only subjective ones. Rather " 'Selves' are socially constructed through language and maintained in narrative" (Freedman & Combs, 1996, p. 34). Consequently, people are able to construct a variety of stories about themselves.

Narrative therapists, in particular Michael White and David Epston (1990), assume "that persons organize and give meaning to their experience through the storying of their lived experience" (p. 12). Narrative therapists refer to dominant narratives versus preferred narratives. The stories people tell about themselves to define themselves are known as dominant stories. In narrative therapy, however, it is possible to change the dominant story for another, preferred reality. White and Epston (1990) contend:

persons are rich in lived experience, that only a fraction of this experience can be storied and expressed at one time, and that a great deal of lived experience falls outside the dominant stories about the lives and relationships of persons. Those aspects of lived experience that fall outside the dominant story provide a rich and fertile source for the generation, or re-generation, of alternate stories. (p. 15)

Tools of Narrative Therapy

In his article "The Promise of Narrative," Bill O'Hanlon (1994) carefully delineates the steps narrative therapists use with their clients to deconstruct dominant stories and to replace them with preferred stories. According to O'Hanlon, one of the first steps in narrative therapy to help restory a person's life is to "come up with a mutually acceptable name for the problem" (p. 25). In doing so, the therapist tries to "linguistically sever" the person from the problem label in order for the person to take on an externalized view of the problem" (pp. 25-26). For narrative therapists, "the person is never the problem; the problem is the problem" (p. 25). By externalizing the problem, separating clients from "problem-saturated descriptions" of life (White & Epston, 1990), people begin to perceive possibilities for themselves in alternate lives or as characters in preferred stories.

In order to separate further the person from the problem, the next step in narrative therapy is to personify the problem by attributing to it negative, oppressive characteristics. Using the figures of speech of metaphor or personification, the therapist might say, for example, "How long has Bulimia been abusing you?" or "When did Depression take over your life?" Lyness and Thomas (1995) speak of the value of using metaphors in therapy:

> Metaphors are empowering and do encourage a sense of authorship in one's life because they are indirect and use abductive learning and transderivational searches. Meaning is generated internally for the client and the client is empowered to find changes in his or her own life. (p.137)

As a result of this linguistic technique, clients and those around them begin to stop identifying the client as the problem. Instead, the negative effects of the problem are attributed to the problem, rather than to the person.

Next, the therapist and client explore the influence of the problem through a series of "externalizing conversations" (White & Epston, 1990). During this externalization process, the therapist usually asks two sets of questions: one set to "map the influence of the problem" in the client's life and the second set to encourage the client to map his or her own influence in the life of the problem (White & Epston, p. 42). For instance, the therapist might ask questions like "When has Jealousy convinced you to do something you regretted later?" or "What kind of lies has Depression been telling you about your worth as a person?" (O'Hanlon, 1994, p. 26). Emphasizing the words "Jealousy" and "Depression" indicates the personification of these two problems. In this process, therapists are particularly careful about the language they use to describe the problem, showing how problems never make a person do something, but rather problems might "influence," "invite," "tell," or "encourage," but never "cause " or "make" people act, thus highlighting people's choice in relationship to the problem.

In addition, in this discussion the therapist looks for times when clients' lives have not been dominated or disrupted by their problems. Instead, the therapist delves for the exceptions, or "unique outcomes," when the problem does not dominate (White & Epston, 1996).

> Unique outcomes include events from the person's lived experience that contradict stories of personal deficits and permanent damage . . . people we have worked with often discover that they decided to come to therapy after having experiences that helped them recognize the possibility that they could make a difference in their lives. . . . They begin to experiment with more preferred stories about themselves and their relationships. (Adams-Wescott & Isenbart, 1996, p. 16)

For the therapist having discovered unique outcomes or exceptions to the problem, the next step in the narrative therapy process is to find additional evidence or examples of times in which to support a new view of the person as competent enough to have stood up to, defeated, or escaped from the dominance or oppression of the problem, so that the client's life story is rewritten. "Narrative therapists use the evidence of discovered competence as a gateway to a parallel universe, one in which the person has a different life story, one in which he or she is competent and heroic" (O'Hanlon, 1994, p. 26). Clients are encouraged to share stories from their past when they have acted strong, brave, and adept. This new story of competence then replaces the problem-saturated story so dominating the client's life. Now that the person is viewed as competent and successful in dealing with the problem, the client and the family are asked to predict the future of this new competent person and to describe what changes will be evident in years to come. For example, the therapist might ask "As you continue to stand up against Anorexia, what do you think will be different about your future than the future Anorexia has planned for you?" (O'Hanlon, p. 26).

Finally, the therapist tries to find or create an audience for perceiving the client's new persona and preferred story. The problem and the solution are set in a social context, because problems are always developed within a social context (Foucault, 1977). Consequently, the therapist might ask the client to write letters to other people who suffer from the same condition, or clients might make a videotape to document their success in overcoming a problem or act as a consultant to others. The client then becomes the expert sharing his or her new view.

Narrative Therapy Tools in a Basic Writing Class

After studying the work of respected narrative therapists, I began to wonder if some of the tools of this type of therapy might be adapted to education as well, in particular with my work with college basic writers in their first composition class in a two-course sequence. For, I knew that many of my students entered the university with stories of academic failure, lacking hope, and never dreaming of the possibility of rewriting their academic stories. I clearly understood that I was not to assume the role of psychological counselor, for neither was I qualified for such a position, nor was the classroom an appropriate arena for such a role. Students with nonacademic problems should be directed to trained counselors. However, because of my expertise in composition instruction, I believed it was appropriate for me to use narratives to provide students with opportunities to make academic progress. Consequently, I decided to try some of the tools of narrative therapy with students enrolled in Learning Support Program (LSP) 080, a ten-week long basic writing class, in the hopes that they would begin to restory their academic lives. I designed a series of writing assignments based on the tools of narrative therapy to accompany other thematically-arranged writing assignments. I felt comfortable using narrative assignments with LSP 080 students because it was their first writing course and it had as its emphasis expository writing as opposed to argument and persuasion. At this time, the university offered to freshmen two pre-college writing courses sponsored by the Department of Learning Support Programs. Students were placed in these courses based on their high school GPAs, their SAT scores, and their scores on a state mandated placement test. Students with the lowest scores were required to enroll in the first course, LSP 080, a course designed to introduce students to academic writing, in particular the expository essay. Students with higher scores were required to enroll in LSP 081, the second class, an exit-level class, with the purpose of teaching students how write argumentative and persuasive essays in direct preparation for English 111, the regular freshman composition course required by the university.

Reconstructing Academic Histories: Deconstructing Myths

To help my students deconstruct the negative academic stories of their academic lives in order to replace them with preferred stories of academic success, I asked them to write a composition detailing their personal academic histories. Students were instructed to interview their parents, other relatives, and teachers to learn more about the their own academic histories. They were encouraged to review various artifacts, such as report cards, picture albums, certificates of honor, scrap books, and yearbooks for evidence to include in their histories. Students were encouraged to bring these documents to class and to share them with their classmates. Student essays were graded according to a rubric that was used to note the completion of the parental interviews, the thoroughness of the written report, and the inclusion of relevant artifacts. Similar assessment rubrics were designed to meet the goals of the other writing exercises as well. In doing this research, it was my hope that through the reconstruction of their academic histories the students would begin to start to deconstruct the misconceptions they held about their lives, to learn from the experiences of others, and to begin to concentrate on their successful experiences.

As I explained the project, I also modeled my process for researching my own academic history, punctuated by various artifacts that I had gathered from my school days. I told them how on a recent visit to my mother's home, I had come across some of my old personal papers, including church records, report cards, newspaper clippings, and some old photographs. One afternoon I reviewed all these papers, and I was relieved to learn that my academic record was not as mediocre as I had remembered. Although I discovered there were some Cs, I also found that there were a good number of As and Bs as well. In particular, my students loved the story about my poor seventh grade writing skills and my fear that my mother would drop me into Miami's Biscayne Bay unless I started to shape up. They loved this story put in the framework that some years later I was able to earn graduate degrees in English. In addition, I shared with them both the time I had fabricated data for a science project contrasted to the time when I had won an award for working with mentally-challenged students. I also shared with them a picture of me deftly manipulating blocks in kindergarten along with a photograph showing me sitting very obviously lonely and unhappy in my bedroom. In other words, I shared with my students evidence of my less than perfect academic past—those times when I had struggled, had been confused, had to find ways to use my weaknesses, or had to compensate with other strengths. My students were surprised, but I suspect relieved to learn that even English teachers have less than stellar academic records, that there are different paths to success, and that many paths can be made acceptable within the academy. The act of sharing my academic story with my class further helped me to shed additional longstanding myths that I had held about myself academically, for in reviewing my records, I learned that I was in general a better student than I recalled, a member of many school organizations including the Latin Club, and admitted to a selective Jesuit College. Talking about my own academic myths (for example, my belief that statistics is hard), I was able instead to substitute a more balanced and accurate view of my academic life, my strengths, and my weaknesses.

Students agreed to interview their parents, relatives, and former teachers in order to reconstruct their academic histories. Along with a written account, many students brought in artifacts that they shared with their classmates. Students wrote essays about a range of experiences, each story filled with both hope and heartache. Many students wrote about their earliest memories of a mother or another relative reading to them, helping, or encouraging them. One student wrote, "I can remember back to the very early years of my life, and there is always this image of my mother standing over me, not scolding, but encouraging." Another recalled "My mother said, 'From the beginning to the end of her pregnancy she read to me.'" Still another student wrote, "Dad always helped me with science class." Students also recalled times when a parent, usually the mother, intervened at school on their behalf. "When my grades started slipping . . . my mother changed me to a school where she knew everyone and I even had a relative who was my teacher. " Or,

> The teacher told my mother I would read but I wasn't comprehending. So they put me into a slow class. My mother didn't think that I deserved to be in that class. She said I would read to her every night, and explain to her what I had read.

Some students described the loss caused by the absence of a parent, usually the father, due to work, separation, or death. "His death effected [sic] me, not only emotionally and physically, but academically as well. Sometimes I acted as if I just didn't care no more." Holly, who always described herself in the third person wrote "Holly never had a father around. He left after a year and a half." In addition, many students missed their mothers who had to work long hours. "Mom started working more hours." Finally, one student was particularly saddened by the death of her best friend's brother.

> Then a tragedy occurred which changed my life forever. My best friend's brother died. High school years were hard for me. It was in eleventh grade that was the hardest. The school work wasn't hard, but my emotional state was giving me some trouble. I didn't talk much. The main problem was that I missed my best and only friend.

Other disturbances, such as moving often, changing schools, or a parent's change in schedule seemed to affect students negatively.

Some students had to overcome physical difficulties as well. "In third grade my grades were interrupted by a sickness that caused me to suffer from heart failure . . ." Or, "I was not on the other kids' level. I can remember the teacher asking me to read a line or sentence and I would start stuttering and the kids started laughing."

Most students reported being excited about starting school, although a few felt underprepared to begin. Some students particularly identified with one teacher who encouraged them to excel. "In kindergarten I was known as the teacher's pet. I loved to help out." Or, "Holly has a vivid memory of the second grade teacher Mrs. Demarco who would always give Holly the additional copies of the lesson she was teaching." Unfortunately, sometimes students had unpleasant experiences with teachers. "In the eleventh grade, my last quarter I failed Latin. The teacher was horrible and intimidating. One day she got in my face and screamed at me . . ."

In their essays, students who had trouble in school noted that some of their troubles began in middle school. Something had happened to douse their initial enthusiasm with learning.

There comes a point in my memory where the fog that keeps those distant memories clouded, begins to let go. It's right about the end of my grade school years. I was not one of the popular kids, if you can believe they even have popular kids in grade school. . . . As I made my way through middle school, where pimples start to plague the faces of so many, I began to slip away from wanting to achieve anything. I felt I had such a bad life that I deserved to act any way I felt like acting.

Another student shared ". . . I had complications in Science and History. I never could get the concept of Science, and I thought History was a bore."

Finally, other students chronicled experiences of slacking off in high school, not fitting in, making bad academic decisions, and working before deciding to attend college. In these same essays, however, students were also able to find evidence of their successes, noting times of academic and athletic achievement and invitations to join clubs and honor societies. "I decided to throw myself into school and after school activities. . . . when I graduated I had 24.5 credits and a 2.8 grading point average. . . . I do believe I did pretty good in school." Another recalled "I was very successful at it [band]. I attended all of the contests and concerts."

From remembering and writing their academic histories, my students, similar to my experience, discovered that there were generally more positive realities in their academic histories than negative ones and through this writing began the process of restorying their academic lives.

Externalizing the Problem

Next, I asked students to reread their academic histories in order to highlight a "milestone" or "key" event or person in their lives. This activity was designed to help students to continue the process of reconstructing their academic histories, a step adapted from narrative therapy, while at the same time further deconstructing their academic myths. Not only did I ask my students to identify those big events in their lives, but I also encouraged them to recall the strategies they had used to overcome their academic problems. For example, I shared with students my difficulties adjusting academically and socially during my first year in college and how I was able to overcome what I thought were permanent failures. In particular, I detailed how I returned home to the watchful eyes of my parents and how I attended the local community college where I was able to regroup, to set parameters for myself, and eventually to experience academic success. As was the experience in writing their academic histories, students identified and shared a range of milestones, or key events or persons. Milestone events for some students included moving to a new state or country. Moving and not speaking or knowing English well was particularly painful for some students, and some native speakers had difficulty with literacy as well: "When I was in grammar school I use [sic] to stumble over my words and hated reading." On the other hand, for some students, moving was a positive experience, "I think a milestone in my life was the move to Georgia from Illinois. I didn't get along with the other kids in my class so it was nice to have a clean slate." Other students wrote about school adjustment problems, "Entering kindergarten as I said, was difficult for me because I was always use [sic] to older children."

Another student recalled:

Up until fourth grade, I felt I was unstoppable. In the fourth grade, they put me in a remedial class for reading. To me it was saying I was slow. My mom helped me understand why I was put there.

Still another student remembered:

The major point in my life concerning education was the year I had to repeat second grade. . . . It has always been a struggle for me to do those things that are ridiscoll [sic] in English. . . . I think that this is a major reason why I am shy today.

On a more positive note, another student wrote of delayed success:

I went to an alternative high school, and something great happened. . . . It caused a sort of metamorphosis outside and in. For the first time in my life I was accepted for who I was, it renewed my drive to beat the odds.

Teachers affected students both negatively and positively.

The key milestone in my life was when my Latin teacher said that I wouldn't pass the class. Before that point everything had come easy to me, but now I had to realize what I had to do was work hard and pass the class. I had to stop extra activities and devote all my time and energy to my work. I certainly believe that this milestone happened in my life to make me strong and realize that hard work pays off."

Other students noted their experiences of overcoming physical and social problems, such as stuttering, as a milestone event. "I learned how to talk slow and calm and now when I read the words just flow." Another student wrote of the burden of his social standing "The first milestone

I can remember overcoming was the myth that I wasn't as good as other people because of social standing."

Parents seemed to have the biggest influence in students' academic lives, both positively and negatively. "My father's death is what devastated me the most. My grades started to decline, and I was in class but I was never there mentally." Another student recalled:

Another milestone was . . . my parents' divorce, and a sort of fall from grace from me . . . I began to see everything from a negative point of view . . . the best decision I ever made . . . was to get away from everything . . . I joined the army and it has totally changed my direction.

Still another student stated, "I didn't realize until now that my mother was a great influence on my academic history. She pushed me to work harder." Or, "My mother would always make me write letters. . . . She left messages or writing on the refrigerator door. . . . I was given diaries for my birthdays." Or, "Mother always encouraged me to read."

Still other students described certain decisions that affected their academic lives ". . . not continuing with college immediately after high school. . . . I need not dwell on the fact that I would be graduating next quarter if I had stayed in school." Or, "I am the first person in my family to go to college. I believe that's one of the things that motivates me." .

As we shared each others' stories in the class, students were amazed by the breadth of their classmates' experiences and moved by others' honesty and strength to overcome what may have seemed unbelievable odds for success for some students. As a result, we emphasized some of the successful strategies they had employed in their pasts: their acknowledgment that no one is perfect, their willingness to start over, to go with their strengths, and to accept that decisions are not always perfect nor permanent. We also talked about the importance of mentors in our lives and the need to master basic literacy skills. Indeed, the class discussions were powerful, and I believe students began to see those unique outcomes or exceptions to the problems in their academic lives.

To help students further externalize the problem, I next asked them to reread their academic history papers, this time to identify and label one of their academic problem areas. In particular, students were encouraged to use metaphors to describe this problem or to personify the problem. In addition, students were asked to describe how they overcame this particular problem. Again, this activity was designed to separate symbolically and linguistically the academic problems from the personal identities of the students. Students eagerly undertook this task and used metaphors and personification to describe their feelings and experiences. Sample expressions are presented below with students' strategies enclosed in parentheses:

Extended freedom began calling my name in the eighth grade. (Because I had more freedom, I got involved in clubs and activities. In order to participate in any extra activities, my grades had to be a C average.)

Delaying school attacks my bank account. (To overcome this I decided to attend school and make money.)

My *slow reading* skills and my *easily being distracted* would put a choke hold on my learning process. (I am in the process of defeating this by slapping distraction back in the face . . .)

I fought with reading *comprehending* day and night. (Every night I don't rest my eyes without reading something and writing.)

My *grade setback* crushed my confidence. That year this major setback spun me around and upside down. I could not grab hold of it and control it. . . . As I grew older it continued to stalk me. (I have had lots of help with overcoming this setback. My mom would take time out of her busy schedule. . . . She would always say that she had confidence in me . . .)

Writing is my worst enemy. (Every time I write a paper I always ask someone to read it.)

My *illness* held me down like a brick holding a piece of paper. (. . . I realize I have a problem. I try eating more, I force myself to go to sleep at a decent time, I also keep up with my homework.)

Stuttering did not want me to read . . . (I overcame stuttering by learning to read and talk slower.)

Reading put a string around my ankle. (I struggle with reading . . . but I go a lot [sic] of help. Math was a subject that I Aced.)

Boys made school work a battle. (. . . mommy put a end to boys . . .)

Not knowing how to *spell* has hit me and knod [sic] me down a few time.

One young woman wrote a poignant essay describing her father's alcoholism, the family's suffering as a result, and his subsequent recovery. Poetically, she began her essay with the excruciatingly accurate metaphor: "Rain started pouring my sixth grade year. . . . My dad starting drinking a lot . . ."

One day in class, in order to separate symbolically students' problems or situations from their lives, students wrote their metaphors or samples of personification on separate pieces of paper and literally and dramatically "tossed them away" into a wastebasket.

Identifying and Using Unique Outcomes to Build New Behavior

The next class exercise was designed to help students find their areas of expertise, another narrative therapy strategy, and to examine the strategies they used to be successful in these areas. The assumptions underlying this activity were that finding evidence of success in various areas would help students rewrite their academic stories, and those skills or strategies required in one area may transfer to academic situations as well. Students reported expertise in a number of areas: dancing, budgeting money, running track, playing football, baseball, volleyball, basketball, soccer, bowling, playing guitar, singing, and drawing. Students also stated that they were good at car washing, communicating with children, listening attentively, seeing the positive side of a negative situation, taking on responsibilities, caring for the elderly, selling insurance, animal training, and being a good friend. One student reported that he was great at procrastinating! Students' enthusiasm for their expertise is represented well in the following response: "One hobby I do very well is math. I first fell in love with math in the 7th grade."

Students were equally successful in detailing the strategies they employed to achieve their expertise in a particular area. These strategies included a determined attitude, frequent practice, learning from others, team work, working on specific skills, persistence, enjoying rewards, making something fun, working hard, and trying other things. One student wrote about learning from failures and starting over again. "It [playing the guitar] started when I was about ten years old when my father introduced me to the acoustic guitar. I soon decided I wanted to play the drums. I failed miserable [sic] at this and I realized I was meant for the guitar." Other students mentioned the importance of having the proper materials (for example, car washing), being organized, concentrating, having patience, and being dependable. In class, we then had discussions to determine how the strategies that students used in one area of their lives might transfer to their academic lives, too. We talked about the importance of a good attitude, having the proper studying materials, using successful students as models, and the importance of practice. In particular, I remember our discussion based on one's student's sharing of her successful basketball techniques:

> I have been very successful because I work hard at the sport that I am involved in at the time. I practice all the time. I even sleep with my basketball. I have gone as far as standing in the tax line dribbling my ball getting on other people's nerves.

Students admired this student's persistence and constant practice but laughed when I suggested that perhaps they should sleep with their English books under their pillows in order to improve their literacy skills!

In a further attempt to assist my students to see themselves as experts, in this case academic experts, and to continue to reframe their academic stories, I asked them to share their experiences with academic writing. It was almost the end of the term, so I requested that they compose a short paper describing how to write a successful essay. Students took to this task eagerly and willingly shared some of the techniques they had learned in class this term. Almost all students offered practical advice on how to write an academic essay; namely, they recommended that writers narrow their subjects, use a limited thesis statement, and include introduction, body and conclusion paragraphs. Furthermore, students talked about the importance of planning before writing, conducting research, including details in the body paragraphs, and revising and proofreading their papers before handing them in. Of more interest, however, was that some students mentioned the techniques that we had discussed in relationship to their nonacademic areas of expertise. In particular, students advised writers to stay focused and to concentrate. "Stay positive. Take breaks and go back to the paper." Another wrote, "Also keep a positive attitude, encourage yourself to do the best you can and stay focus [sic]."

Others remembered the importance of "practice" and related this strategy to their writing processes. "The old saying 'Practice makes perfect,' doesn't hurt either. So do a lot of writing and practice your techniques or strategies on writing an A essay paper." Or, "First of all, we can practice our writing skills more. The more we write, the better our writings turn out."

Other students mentioned the importance of models or mentors and advised seeking help from a lab tutor or trusted family member or friend. "Then we should ask our friends and family how they feel about the topic." Or, "I take my paper to Mrs. Pat, my English tutor in Kell Hall. She always helps me think about better ways to say what I'm thinking."

Finally, a positive, confident tone was evidenced in student papers. Students were now writing and offering advice from a position of strength, not one of deficit. As evidence, notice the confident tone of one student's advice:

> May I suggest outlines, mapping and jotting information. . . . Try to stay positive. . . . Second, keep the reader interested. Try asking a question in your intro that will be answered in your body paragraphs. Use a little quote or a controversial remark to get the reader's eye jumping. Establish the importance of your subject.

Another said, "These technique are the most effective from my experience in writing essays." And, finally another student recommended the following practical advice:

> Do not babble. If you find yourself babbling, or prolonging the topic, do not hesitate to stop yourself before you have written more than that's [sic] needed. If a writer is babbling, his or her audience may start to become bored.

Restorying and Reframing Experience

The last major narrative therapy type of exercise of the quarter was developed to reinforce students' new sense of competency by finding an audience for them to share their new identities. For this purpose, students were asked to write letters to prospective Learning Support freshmen advising them how to succeed in the university and in their Learning Support classes. In an interview, David Epston speaks to the value of this practice ". . . in this therapy, people emerge as heroes, and they often want the heroism acknowledged in some social way. They are usually quite happy to communicate with others in some social way" (O'Hanlon, 1994, p. 28).

Students offered a wide range of advice concerning the university as a whole and Learning Support Program courses in particular. They described various university facilities including the University Center, campus restaurants, and the Pullen Library, and they advised students to avail themselves of university services such as the Learning Support Programs and Special Services. They recommended asking other students for the names of good professors. "LS ___ was my worst class, but it was a helpful course. I say it was my worst because my professor was VERY unorganized. So make sure you find a good professor." Furthermore, students discussed problems with registration and recommended registering over the phone and provided study skills pointers: "Don't cram for tests. Follow the syllabus. Come to class. Be on time." Other students discussed the importance of getting involved on campus and the advantages of joining clubs. "This university has many clubs, activities, and sports available . . . Get involved because this university is a downtown campus, it is what you make of it." A few students remarked positively about the diversity of the university's student body. ". . . this university has a diversity of nationalities, and this alone prepares a student for the multi-cultural, real world."

Students were particularly empathetic to the incoming students and their Learning Support placement. "As a LSP student I can understand some of the feelings you are probably feeling at this moment. You are saying to yourself that you do not belong in this program." Or, another student shared:

> At first, I was reluctant about being in a LSP class because I didn't want anyone to think I was not smart. . . . Do not get discouraged or weary, just consider the Learning Support Program as a firm foundation that is being built to make sure you are successful in college.

Or, "Even if you have to take learning support classes do not be ashamed because they were very helpful. I, myself was in learning support classes and feel better because I took them." Some students then went on to explain some of the complexities of Learning Support placement: "I am sure that you are wondering why you were placed in this class but don't fret the professors will be happy to explain it to you."

Finally, most students promised the incoming students that these classes would help them in the long run. "The most important fact that I need to tell you is that you will only get out of these classes what you put into them." Another student consolingly remarked

> but take it from me, a former learning support student, these classes will only help you. In these classes I have learned more about the University from the library to programs given. I would have never learned these in other classes.

Still another student wrote, "LSP courses will help you in a lot of classes. It will strengthen our background and format for English 111." Other positive comments included: "I never thought I would never [sic] be more proud to have taken learning support classes. I thought these classes were for remedial students, but they were not." Or,

> Many good things can come out of being in this program. If you are smart you will take my advice and use this class as a stepping stool and take all the information out of them [sic] as you can.

Some students offered some general advice for success "Just don't give up, because everything is not easy," while others provided advice on how to succeed in composition classes, in particular:

> When you enter this class just be aware you are going to write and write and write some more. If you feel you can not [sic] write papers do not worry you don't have a choice. Continue to write and she will continue to grade. After a few papers you will get use [sic] to the grading scale . . .

Or, "During the quarter there is a debate. All though it does require effort it is nothing that will kill you." Or, "My teacher's name was Dr. . . . She loves it when students call her doctor."

Truly, these last papers reflect the students' feelings of accomplishment, competence, and hope. These Learning Support students no longer viewed themselves as failures, "students in Loser Sciences classes," but rather as students who have climbed just one of the many steps needed to complete their college educations successfully.

Reflections: Narrative Therapy Tools in a College Basic Writing Class

The question guiding this practice was whether or not the tools from narrative therapy might be adapted for use in classes with college basic writers. Based on my experience and my students' work, I believe that narrative therapy techniques can be powerful change agents in assisting students to restory their academic lives. My experience with this class leads me to believe that these techniques might be used to help improve students' academic self-confidence. Not only might these exercises increase students' self-esteem, they also provide authentic writing assignments to be written for real audiences–themselves, their classmates, and future students. Students moved from writing personal narratives at the beginning of the term to writing expository assignments by the end of the term, as evidenced in their advice papers. These final papers seemed to indicate that they students were attitudinally ready to move on to the second-level basic writing class where they would work on perfecting composition skills appropriate for regular college courses. They seemed to have assumed a different way of being–a more positive, self-assured stance—which hopefully leads to improved academic writing.

Selected tools from narrative therapy may be adapted for use in a basic college composition classroom. A course or a curriculum based on the philosophy and techniques of narrative therapy will have many components and versions. Foremost, however, teachers must subscribe to one of the main tenets of narrative therapy: "the person is never the problem; [rather], the problem is the problem" (O'Hanlon, 1994, p. 24). Poor literacy skills should never be personified as the students sitting in front of us. Rather, classroom teachers might emulate Baker and Steiner (1995), who when working with students suffering from writers' block, "normalize" the experience by sharing those times when they, like many of their students, "go blank." Next, they recommend professors seek the students' advice, asking them to describe when and in what situations their ideas flowed more freely. Through this dialogue, students have their experiences validated and can rely on those positive experiences, those times when ideas flowed freely, to help them in the future when they are asked to write on demand.

Narrative therapists (Adams-Wescott & Isenbart, 1996; Madigan, 1996; White & Epston, 1990) are also careful not to separate the personal from the political and believe that all stories are based on cultural stories. Foucault (1977) writes about the power of language and how people's power in a particular society is based on their ability to participate in various discourses of this society. Madigan (1996) explains the narrative therapist's view of the influence and power of the dominant culture when he writes:

> The focus of our therapy is to render transparent the discourse and status of identity-based politics in the life of a problem (gender, race, class), and the effects these discourse practices have had on a person's relationships. Persons are not viewed as fixed within problem identities: a person's identity is viewed with the politics and power plays of a culturally manufactured and constituted self. (p. 50)

Freedman and Combs (1996) concur: "Whether or not one consciously owns one's beliefs and behaviors as related to a political stance, they are political in their 'real effects' " (p.46; italics are in the original).

There are many ways to examine the power of the dominant culture over a person and its contributions to a person's problems, whether personal or academic. Class discussions, and oral and written narratives can diffuse the influence of various social constructs. Sondra Perl (1994) asks her literature students "But how, I wonder, do we see beyond the boundaries of a familiar story and envision a new one: What, in other words, are the connections between the texts we read and the lives we live, between composing our stories and composing ourselves?" (p. 427). Reading literature, in particular, biographies and autobiographies, is helpful in providing models of people who have successfully restoried their lives. Texts that have generated positive feedback in my writing classroom include Mike Rose's *Lives on the Boundary* (1989), *The Autobiography of Malcolm X* (Malcolm X, Haley, & Handler, 1964), Sandra Cisneros' *House on Mango Street* (1984), Pat Conroy's *The Great Santini* (1976), and Maya Angelou's *I Know Why the Caged Bird Sings* (1970). Inviting guest speakers to class, those who have restoried their own lives, provides both role models and mentors for students who are looking for direction.

White and Epston (1990) also recommend using "counter documents" to support people's new descriptions of themselves. In particular, they suggest the use of letters, certificates, and declarations. Teachers, too, might write letters to their students agreeing upon an action plan for a particular situation, or at the end of the academic term, they might write letters detailing the students' accomplishments in a class, or award certificates to successful students at the end of a course.

Finally, it must be reiterated that English teachers cannot and should not assume the role of professional therapists, counseling students about personal problems. Instructors should recommend that students discuss these personal problems with trained counselors, and teachers can provide resources for students. Instructors should also be sensitive to the privacy needs of the students. Some students may not feel comfortable revealing their academic woes and should not be forced. Instead, alternate assignments might be provided or students should be presented topic options within each major assignment. Instructors must also be careful to balance the coverage of both narrative and expository themes and techniques. Furthermore, it cannot be claimed that the use of the narrative therapy techniques can improve students' academic writing. Instead, instructors might assume the philosophy and use the techniques of narrative therapy to help their students to deconstruct the myths they hold about themselves as students and their misconceptions about their academic lives. As a result, students might begin to view themselves in a new light, one filled with hope, confidence, and success.

Note: Special thanks to my colleague, Nancy Chase for introducing me to narrative therapy and sharing her thoughts concerning the linkages between narrative therapy and academic success.

References

Adams-Wescott, J., & Isenbart, D. (1996). Creating preferred relationships: The politics of recovery from child sexual abuse. *Journal of Systemic Therapies, 15*(1), 13-31.

Anderson, H., & Goolishian, H. (1988). Human systems as linguistic systems: Preliminary and evolving ideas about the implications for clinical theory. *Family Process,27*, 371-393.

Angelou, M. (1970). *I know why the caged bird sings*. New York: Random House.

Bean, J.P., & Metzner, B.S. (1985). A conceptual model of nontraditional undergraduate attrition. *Review of Educational Research, 55*, 485-540.

Baker, M.R., & Steiner, J.R. (1995). Solution-focused social work. Metamessages to students in higher education opportunity programs. *Social Work, 40*, 225-232.

Berger, P., & Luckmann, T. (1966). *The social construction of reality*. New York: Doubleday.

Broughton, V.J. (1986, June). *A causal analysis of attrition at an urban non-residential university*. Paper presented at the meeting of the Association for Institutional Research, Orlando, FL.

Bruner, J. (1991). The narrative construction of reality. *Critical Inquiry, 18*, 1-21.

Cisneros, S. (1984). *The house on Mango Street*. New York: Vintage Books.

Conroy, P. (1976). *The great Santini*. Boston: Houghton Mifflin.

Foucault, M. (1977). *Discipline and punishment: The birth of the prison*. Middlesex, UK: Peregrine Books.

Freedman, J. & Combs, G. (1996). *Narrative therapy: The social construction of preferred realities*. New York: W.W. Norton.

Lyness K. & Thomas, V. (1995). Fitting a square peg in a square hole: Using metaphor in narrative therapy. *Contemporary Family Therapy, 17*, 127-142.

Madigan, S. (1996). The politics of identity: Considering community discourse in the externalizing of internalized problem communities. *Journal of Systemic Therapies, 15*(1), 47-63.

O'Hanlon, B. (1994). The third wave. *Family Therapy Networker, 18*(6), 18-49.

Perl, S. (1994). Composing texts, composing lives. *Harvard Educational Review, 64*, 427-449.

Rose, M. (1989). *Lives on the boundary*. New York: Macmillan.

Tinto, V. (1993). *Leaving college: Rethinking the causes and cures of student attrition*. Chicago: The University of Chicago.

White, M., & Epston, D. (1990). *Narrative means to therapeutic ends*. New York: W.W. Norton.

X, Malcolm, Haley, A., & Handler, M.S. (1964). *The autobiography of Malcolm X*. New York: Random House.

Developing Writers Using Technology

Patsy Krech
University of Memphis

Abstract

Developmental educators are facing the challenge of teaching courses on-line. Some teachers insist that basic and developmental students cannot succeed in on-line courses; however, other teachers believe that on-line instruction can benefit developmental students. This chapter shows how one approach to an on-line course proved to be successful in both the instructor's and the students' estimation. If a writing course is structured and designed with developmental students in mind, it can teach both the writing skills and the technology that students need.

In Fall 1999 I taught a section of basic composition as an on-line course, the first attempt for a developmental studies writing course on-line at our university. As I considered creating such a course, I was reluctant for several reasons. Having taught developmental studies writing courses for over 20 years, I am aware that many developmental students need teacher instruction, enthusiasm, motivation, and interaction, and I feared that the lack of personal, face-to-face contact between student and teacher would result in poor work or no work submitted. Over the past few years, I developed web pages to accompany my courses with syllabi, assignments, links to helpful web sites, and other information. Because students in my courses often did not know how to access these sources or to use e-mail, in 1997 I began taking all of my composition students to a computer training lab for one class session to show them how to access

For additional information contact: Patsy Krech • University of Memphis • Transitional Academic Studies • Administration Building #203 • Memphis, TN 38152 • e-mail: pakrech@memphis.edu the web site and to send e-mail. Based on that experience and on students' responses to surveys during those semesters, I knew that students in my courses generally did not have even basic computer skills. Only a few had used Microsoft Word, e-mail, or the Internet, and most did not have a computer at home. To take an on-line course, they would have to use computer labs on campus and learn the required computer skills. In addition to my reluctance about my students' ability and motivation was my lack of knowledge. Although I have progressed steadily with my computer knowledge and abilities since I first touched a personal computer in 1993 (with high anxiety at the time), I realized that I would have to learn to use programs available to students in our computer labs: Netscape Mail and a courseware program to post all the course materials on the web. An on-line course seemed like a daunting assignment for me and for my students. However, I accepted the challenge and began to design the course.

Course Design

After introductory workshops in our faculty computer training center, I learned through trial and error to use Netscape Mail and CourseInfo. Using the syllabus for a traditional section of basic writing, I created units of assignments and activities. I decided that students should work certain exercises in the textbook for the course, *Grassroots: The Writer's Workbook* (Fawcett & Sandberg, 1997). The answers for most of these exercises would be available on the CourseInfo site for students to check their work; then they would send one or two review exercises each week to me by e-mail, and I would respond with an explanation of items missed. As a review for the skills in the exercises, I created a quiz for each week, using the CourseInfo quiz generator. Next, I had to decide between an asynchronous approach and a more campus-structured course. In traditional sections of basic composition, I teach students grammar, spelling, and mechanics in the context of writing. For example, in preparation for narrative writing, students work with past tense verbs, direct and indirect quotations, and quotation marks. They write a rough draft out of class and bring it to a "workshop" day to write a final draft while I am available to answer questions about their writing. To allow for such exchanges in the on-line section and to continue this process approach toward writing, I decided on a "primarily on-line" format. For about half of the weeks during the semester, the students would submit their paragraphs through e-mail, and I would respond to them, correcting mistakes, commenting on content, organization, and development, and giving a sample grade when appropriate. The format for the course was similar to Personalized System of Instruction (PSI; Keller, 1968). Keller's learning system stressed written course materials instead of the more traditional lecture method. For this on-line course, students received information about writing skills in writing, through CourseInfo handouts and e-mail from the instructor. Other important aspects of PSI include self-pacing by students and mastery learning (Keller, 1968). Students determined when to do assignments within the confines of the deadlines for the course. Usually, they had a week during which to accomplish a unit's assignments. Because of the asynchronous design of the course, students could complete assignments in the middle of the afternoon or night even though the course time was in the morning. If students needed more practice to master writing skills, I would recommend specific web sites or create handouts to post in CourseInfo or interactive quizzes through web pages I found. In addition to the activities and exercises, the students would come to our assigned classroom four times during the semester to write a final draft of a composition for a grade, with the option of asking me questions about their writing. Also, they would take the final exam in the same situation as all other basic writing students, in class with two hours to plan and write a composition.

Initially, 20 students enrolled in the on-line section, which had a notation in the schedule of classes as "primarily on-line." In a preliminary survey on the first day of class, all of the students stated that they did not realize this section was an on-line course. The notation was evidently too easy to overlook. I explained the approach the course was to take and encouraged them to enroll in a traditional class if that was what they preferred. No one dropped until a couple of weeks later when one student withdrew from all classes, and another student withdrew from this one only. Thus, the final enrollment was 18.

For the next four scheduled class meetings, I conducted training in a computer lab on campus. I showed students how to open their university accounts and demonstrated how to use Microsoft Word, Netscape Mail, and my web pages. Students enrolled themselves in the CourseInfo site for our course and learned how to take on-line quizzes and how to access assignment schedules and course handouts on that site. After the introduction to technology, the students embarked on their on-line learning. For several weeks they worked on assignments and sent e-mails to me with writing assignments and exercises. They took quizzes and accessed web pages for grammar and composition help. About every other week they returned to our classroom to produce a final draft of a writing assignment. During these sessions they asked me about problems they were having with their writing. Some came to my office for additional instruction or sent e-mails with their inquiries.

Course Evaluation

On a final course survey, students indicated that they had learned the course material well or very well. All but one student indicated the desire to take another on-line course. When asked what they had learned in this course, they listed writing skills such as commas, sentence punctuation, and subject verb agreement. In fact, these students' writings compared favorably with those of students in traditional classes. Their writing demonstrated improvement in specific development and organization, as well as in areas of grammar, spelling, and punctuation. Through sending e-mails related to assignments, students received even more writing practice, and in a real world manner. They quickly realized that their e-mail messages must ask clearly and concisely what they needed to know about a writing assignment or about grammar for the instructor's response to be helpful. Several students also said they had learned to manage their time more effectively and to read assignments more accurately. Thus, the course enhanced students' skills as independent learners and gave them the opportunity to be more in charge of their learning experience. Stahl, Simpson, and Hayes (1992) identified the need to become more independent and responsible learners as one important factor for developmental students to change if they are to succeed in college.

One predictable outcome of the course was that students learned more about technology. Although a few students knew how to use Microsoft Word, e-mail, and the Internet prior to taking the class, the majority, 14 of the original 20 students, indicated having little knowledge of these technologies. By the end of the course, students believed that they had acquired proficiency in all of the computer skills they had utilized. With the current emphasis on real-world assignments and skills, computer technology is important for students in college and for future employment. Trimble (1999) cites the need for instruction that fosters the appropriate technology to prepare students for the business world. Students also learned to ask for technical support from me or from lab staff, thus acquiring communication and self-advocacy skills that created good habits for the future. At times, I sent detailed instructions, at students' request, to explain how to do some computer task, such as sending an attachment or changing font color. Reading and following directions taught them the need for accuracy and process in writing. While searching for sources with writing, punctuation, and grammar practices on the Internet, students recognized the need for valid and reliable web sites. In addition to learning more about writing, my students reported that they became more proficient in e-mailing, web surfing, and word processing.

Although I originally designed this course with reluctance, I now appreciate the power of teaching on-line. The combination of asynchronous learning and on-campus meetings worked well for these students. Of the 20 originally enrolled, 16 passed, 2 withdrew, and 2 failed. These statistics are consistent with traditional courses taught by the same instructor. Also, students viewed the course as successful. In fact, at the request of several of the students, I agreed to teach the subsequent course, developmental writing, on-line the following semester. Nine of the students in the basic on-line writing course enrolled in the developmental course and passed it. The critical test for this basic writing course will come when the students enroll in freshmen level courses. Tracking them should show whether or not the course prepared them for college-level writing.

Recommendations

Faculty choosing to teach on-line should carefully consider the technologies to use. If the software or computer tasks are too difficult, students may become discouraged. The high failure rate reported for many on-line courses may be caused in part by such frustration. Computer training seems essential for most students to ensure their ability to complete assignments. One student who failed the on-line course attended only one of the training sessions, and one who withdrew attended only two. Furthermore, establishing procedures for selecting on-line students may increase success rates. The second student who received an F had failed basic composition the previous semester in a traditional course because of poor attendance and failure to submit assignments. Students who have exhibited a lack of self-motivation are probably not good candidates for an on-line course. In an attempt to enroll students, some instructors or institutions have created criteria for students to use in determining their preparedness for on-line instruction. A method that might encourage students to persist in the course would be to add synchronous communication to an on-line course, such as chat rooms. These technologies may increase students' feelings of community and connectedness in the course.

Another issue for faculty to consider in preparing to teach on-line is students' access to computers. Some colleges require students to own their own computer with certain capabilities before they enroll in an on-line course. Others may recommend that on-line students have their own computers because the number of computers on their campus is limited. Especially for synchronous courses, owning a personal computer may be a necessity because this type of course does not require students to come to campus for their learning experience. Research shows that students from low-income and minority backgrounds are less likely to own or to have used a computer, so on-line courses "may deepen the divide between the educational haves and have-nots" (Gladieux & Swail, 1999, p. 8). However, if a campus has sufficient computer access and if the instructor teaches technologies in addition to the content of the course, an asynchronous course can serve to bridge the divide for lower income and minority students. In my on-line course, only a few students had a computer at home, and they reported that the university had enough computers so that they could access one without difficulty. The students who did not have a computer at home would probably not have learned how to use one during this semester if they had not taken this on-line course. Teaching them the technologies for the course provided them with the opportunity to learn computer skills that they might not have otherwise mastered. By the end of the course, several of the students told me they hoped to buy a computer in the next year or so.

Conclusion

I set out on this journey in an effort to develop basic writers by using technology as the method of delivery. At first, I hesitated because the technology or the distance might be a hindrance. Instead, students used the technology in ways that increased their learning potential and developed skills that should make them better college students and better candidates for future employers. I plan to continue teaching on-line because both the students and I found the approach to be successful.

References

Fawcett, S., & Sandberg, A. (1997). *Grassroots: The writer's workbook* (4th ed.). Boston: Houghton Mifflin.

Gladieux, L., & Swail, W. (1999). *The virtual university and educational opportunity: Issues of equity and access for the next generation*. [On-Line]. Available: http://www.collegeboard.org/index_this/policy/html/April.pdf

Keller, F. (1968). Goodbye teacher.... *Journal of Applied Behavior Analysis, 1*, 79-89.

Stahl, N., Simpson, M., & Hayes, C. (1992). Ten recommendations from research for teaching at risk college students. *Journal of Developmental Education, 16*(4), 2-10.

Trimble, S. (1999). *Refocusing teacher education: 21st century teacher competencies and related factors.* Paper presented at the annual meeting of the World Future Society, Washington, DC (ERIC Document Reproduction Service No. 434875)

Stigma

Mark Pedelty
University of Minnesota

Abstract

Thirty-eight students conducted ethnographic research among their peers at South Haven (pseudonym), a developmental program within a large public university. The students found that many of their peers feel stigmatized. This chapter will explore possible sources and meanings of students' feelings of stigma within institutional and wider cultural contexts. The author argues that stigmatization is an inevitable outcome of academic ranking and a result of the ideological narratives driving U.S. education. He proposes a "justice model" to deal with issues of academic stigma among students and faculty in developmental education programs.

"I am disappointed to be in South Haven because it is considered by students in other colleges to be a high school, a place for kids who are not smart enough to be in their colleges." — South Haven Student

I have been teaching and conducting research for the past year in a developmental program, which I will call South Haven. One year of research and teaching in developmental education hardly qualifies me to draw definitive conclusions about the field. I liken myself to the "parachuters" in the international press corps. Such reporters are famous for popping into a

For additional information contact: Mark Pedelty • General College • University of Minnesota • 260 Appleby Hall • 128 Pleasant St. SE • Minneapolis, MN 55455 • e-mail: pedeltmh@umn.edu country during a flare-up, jotting off a few superficial news reports for the home audience, and then taking off. Local and resident foreign reporters resent the hell out of these interlopers for claiming to be authorities when they are little more than tourists. More often than not, parachute reporting is superficial and, quite often, riddled with errors.

I conducted an ethnographic study of a foreign press corps, living among and studying them for well over a year. In addition to discovering the depths of resentment felt by the local corps for their parachuting colleagues, however, I learned that even the most angered resident reporters found at least some value in the parachuters' prose. That value, in a nutshell, was summed up by the term "fresh eyes." Despite their Banana Republic pretense, these parachuters could at least recognize the unusual elements of a local story, noticing things that those living there had begun to ignore. In the case of the country I was studying, for example, parachuters would exhibit surprise and revulsion at the violence that pervaded the country. The resident corps had mostly become inured to the violence, and had difficulty writing about it for the home audience, whereas the parachuters were able to maintain the fresh eyes and pen of the naïve outsider (Pedelty, 1995).

I am both an ethnographer and parachuter in the field of developmental education. Therefore, I am certain that some of my observations will be either banal or miss the mark altogether. My hope, however, is that my ethnographic training and fresh eyes have allowed me to deal with at least one topic that the resident corps, in this case veteran developmental education professionals, may be overlooking: stigma. Since my first semester at South Haven, I have been struck by both the level of stigma felt by many of our students, and the lack of attention to the issue in the developmental education literature. As a cultural anthropologist, I am fascinated by such phenomena, issues that pattern behavior, yet rarely become part of overt social discourse.

South Haven operates as part of a larger, public research university. Previously, I taught the academic elite, including undergraduates with high entering grade point averages and exceptional test scores. Throughout the year, I have found myself drawing comparisons between these past teaching experiences and my current work at South Haven. The most obvious areas of divergence have to do with curriculum and class size, rather than differences in students. South Haven students' reading, writing, and math skills are, on average, only slightly less developed than those of students I have taught at highly selective institutions. Plus, South Haven students exhibit an incredible range of untapped talents. Furthermore, they seem to "catch-up" relatively quickly during the course of the year, demonstrating that it is not anything inside the students that differentiates them from my students at highly selective institutions, but rather something in their prior educational experience that has made it difficult for them to succeed.

However, there is one very striking difference between my students at South Haven and those I previously taught. South Haven students exhibit and express a strong sense of stigmatization, a feeling that others, particularly other students, consider them inferior. I encountered this even before starting to teach at South Haven. A local hardware store employee told me South Haven is "where they put all the dumb kids." A few months later, just after starting the fall semester, I overheard a South Haven student talking to a friend: "So, they put you in the retard college too?" I have read and heard many such statements during my first year at South Haven.

I first realized the depth of the South Haven stigma when I asked my students to help me redesign Introduction to Cultural Anthropology to better fit their needs. To start the process, I asked them to tell me about their South Haven experiences, in general. One by one, the majority of students complained South Haven was "not really college," but rather a sort of remedial high school in the midst of what, by implication, was a "real college." Many stated they either felt, or were made to feel, intellectually inferior.

Fortunately, several students, including a few from the real college, made statements in support of South Haven. They noted the diversity of the student body, small class sizes, and close contact with the professor as advantages of South Haven compared to the university as a whole. Yet, the overall tone was one of self-doubt, embarrassment, stigma, and not a little anger regarding provisional admittance to the university. Believing these issues to be worthy of further research, I dedicated the next semester's class research project to ethnographic study of South Haven student culture.

Our collaborative investigation raised more questions than it answered. However, one result was unequivocal. Rightly or wrongly, a large percentage of South Haven students believe that other students in the university look down on them. In other words, they feel stigmatized.

Literature

A recent commentary by Jeanne Higbee (2000) captures the problem well: "One of the greatest challenges of developmental education is eliminating the stigma associated with programs designed to enhance academic achievement" (p. 41). The potential sources of such stigma range from state legislatures (Hardin, 1998) to peers. In some cases it may simply be self-inflicted. Regardless of where it comes from, it is real. Stigma is part of the cultural matrix within which we teach and learn.

Unfortunately, there is relatively little discussion of stigma in the developmental education literature. Valeri-Gold, Callahan, Deming, Mangram, and Errico (1997) completed one of the few research projects to touch on the question. They surveyed 125 students concerning their educational attitudes, hopes, dreams, fears, and expectations as students in a developmental program. When asked, "How are you feeling about being a student at the university?" Of the 125 responses, 51 were rated as generally negative after the first month of classes. As a result, Valeri-Gold and colleagues determined that "negative perceptions of developmental studies persist and interfere with student learning" (p. 15).

The Valeri-Gold study is rare, however. Although there are numerous studies of the stigma felt by students who are disabled (Low, 1996), persons of color (Brown, 1998; Castro, 1974; Gilbert, 1998), gay (Smith, 1998), low income (Miller & Evko, 1985; Schafer, Olexa, & Polk, 1970; Wiltfang & Scarbecz, 1990;), speak English as a second language (Kamwangamalu, 1997), or have a history of psychiatric hospitalization (Dougherty et al., 1996), there has been very little research on feelings of stigma among college students in developmental programs. Given that many of the students in developmental education programs belong to the above categories, it stands to reason that the negative stereotypes applied to these student populations would overlap with, and feed into, the stigma applied to students in developmental programs. Barry Castro (1974) found this to be the case for students of the Maria de Hostos Community College in New York, which gained the derogatory nickname, "Ghetto College." The same appellation is occasionally used in reference to South Haven, demonstrating that the stigma applied to developmental programs is not solely a result of provisional admittance or academic "failure," but rather recognition that a large percentage of students of color are enrolled in such programs. In other words, there is a strong element of racism in the stigma attached to developmental programs.

The relative lack of research and publication concerning stigma is understandable, when one considers the environment within which developmental educators work. There is a general fear of discussing potentially negative aspects of developmental programs, which have enough enemies as it is. Likewise, there is a tendency to confuse advocacy and scholarship in the developmental literature due to the perceived need to promote as well as study our programs. Therefore, as one colleague explained, stigma "is something we talk about, but we don't really write about it." I hope that by writing about it, however, we might find more effective ways to deal with the problem.

Method

I asked my students to conduct an ethnographic study of South Haven. There were 38 students in the class by the end of the semester. Over half of the students speak English as a second language (ESL), which seems to have affected the results somewhat. Most of the ESL students are enrolled in South Haven due to language test scores rather than their performance on standardized tests or high school grades.

To begin, each student chose a South Haven classmate to interview concerning a range of educational and cultural issues. Some of these partners were also enrolled in the course; others were from outside the class. About half of the students chose ESL students. Following the model of Anna Deveare-Smith (1993), I then asked the students to write and perform monologues based on these ethnographic interviews. We filmed the monologues for further investigation and presentation.

I listed seven groups of potential questions in the assignment guide, but encouraged students to let their South Haven informants dictate the development of the interview:

1. Would you please give me a general outline of your life history? Where are you from and where have you lived? What do the members of your family do for a living? What have been the most important events in your life to this point?

2. Tell me about your educational background. Where did you receive your education? How do you feel about the educational institutions that you have experienced? Which areas of study

have you succeeded in? What made you succeed in those areas? Which areas of study have you been the least successful in? Why do you feel that you have had less success in those areas? How have extracurricular activities (including employment) affected your education? How did your peers affect your education? How did your family influence your educational career?

3. Why are you in South Haven? What were your other options, and why did you choose South Haven? How do you feel about being assigned to South Haven?

4. Describe and evaluate your educational experience at South Haven thus far. Have you gained a lot from South Haven? What are some of the positive aspects of South Haven? What are some of the negative aspects? How do you feel about being a South Haven student? What advice would you give to someone who is thinking of enrolling in South Haven next year?

5. Describe South Haven student culture. What types of interactions do you experience with South Haven students in the classroom? What types of interactions do you experience with students outside the classroom? What types of interactions do you observe inside the classroom? What types of student interactions do you observe outside the classroom? Are there subcultures (e.g., interest groups, cohorts arranged by ethnicity, cliques, etc.) within the South Haven student body? Are you part of any of these subcultures or subgroups? Describe your subculture or subgroup. Why do you belong to this subgroup, and how does it influence your educational experience? Describe other subcultures or subgroups and their interactions with other South Haven students. In general, how do you feel about your peers in the South Haven? How do you think that you are perceived by University students who are not South Haven majors? How do you think the South Haven is perceived by students outside of the South Haven? Does this perception influence your feelings about yourself as a student? Does this perception influence your feelings about yourself as a person, in general?

6. Where do you plan to go after the South Haven? Are you planning on transferring to another college or another university? If so, what are you going to major in? What are your career plans?

7. Thank you for allowing me to interview you. I am going to select certain responses in order to craft a monologue and performance. I will submit the monologue to you before showing it to anyone else. You will have complete editorial control. If there is anything that you would like to delete or add, you will have the opportunity to do so. Please note that I will be performing this monologue in front of my class, and it might be filmed for inclusion in a documentary film about the South Haven. Would you prefer that use your real name, or would you prefer that I apply a pseudonym for the monologue and performance? You will have the ability to modify elements in the monologue to disguise your identity, if you so choose.

Question clusters 3 through 5 were the most likely to elicit responses concerning stigma.

Results

Of the 38 interview monologues, 25 dealt with issues of stigma. (It should be noted that two of the informants were not South Haven students but rather students from other colleges who had taken South Haven classes). Many of the students noted their extreme disappointment upon discovering they had been assigned to South Haven rather than to their college of choice in the university. Several described the actual moment when they opened their admissions notice. For example, one explained: "I felt disappointed because my friends said the people who study in South Haven are below average." Another explained: "I was upset that I wasn't accepted into the College of Liberal Arts, but I wasn't surprised." A third stated: "I received a letter that I was accepted to the university, into South Haven. My first reaction was disappointment. I was sad and disappointed to be in South Haven." I have repeatedly encountered this narrative when talking to South Haven students, down to the detail of the admission letter.

The majority of student-informants believe their peers in other programs and people in the wider community hold negative perceptions of South Haven and its students. A few examples:

"Unfortunately, I feel that students outside of South Haven look at us as less astute."

...sometimes it is a little embarrassing. A little embarrassing because when people ask me what college at the U I am attending, I'd say South Haven and they would ask me why I wasn't in (The College of Liberal Arts) or some other college instead, like it wasn't something I should be proud of.

"I got stuck in South Haven because my first choice (The College of Liberal Arts) didn't work out. The reputation of South Haven is that it is easier than other colleges."

At first, I felt so embarrassed when all of my friends asked me which college I was in. This is due to the assumption that South Haven students are not very good and they didn't have any success in high school. Also, the courses in South Haven tend to be more elementary than other colleges offer. These myths reduced my motivation for learning and caused me some problems during my first semester.

"My Dad's friends think that South Haven is not really good and the people there are below average."

"I do feel that other colleges within the university have a bad impression of South Haven students. I think that they think we might be slow, dumb, or did not do well in high school."

"Looking on the outside in, it looks like high school...The students in other colleges seem to look down on it. They don't take South Haven students seriously."

"My perspective on South Haven's student culture, student identities, sociolinguistic categories, formal and informal rituals, etc. is 'Ghetto College'... 'South Haven High'...take your pick...That is how I am seen and how I view South Haven."

Fortunately, many of these same informants expressed positive views concerning their educational experience at South Haven. For example, almost all of the students expressed positive views concerning the multicultural aspect of South Haven. However, such positive assessments were, in turn, balanced in several cases by negative critiques concerning infantilizing aspects of the program, including the close monitoring of student progress, "easy classes," the inability to work directly in one's major, and a lack of class choice. As noted in the following section, these negative qualities were associated with "high school," a category that is understood as the antithesis of "real college." The larger university is, conversely, perceived as real college.

Finally, it should be noted that ESL students tended to present much more positive views of South Haven than their peers. It is possible that the cause of a student's provisional assignment may make a difference. Students assigned to South Haven for linguistic reasons may feel less academic stigma than those admitted because of lower test scores and grades. Future research efforts may shed more light on that and other cohort questions.

Overall, this study is too limited, in terms of quantitative sampling, to draw generalizations to the student population as a whole. However, as an ethnographer, my aim was to achieve cultural depth rather than numerical breadth. This survey data is only a small representation of the ethnographic encounter that took place between the students and myself over the course of the year.

As an anthropologist, my goal was to learn from my students, to understand their perspectives on the local culture. Likewise, having conducted larger scale surveys on more easily quantifiable questions, such as the relationship between media consumption and grades, I must question the value of statistical methodologies for studying issues like educational stigma. It is a cultural problem, involving depth of meaning. Therefore, qualitative, interpretive, and intersubjective methodologies like participant observation are more likely to yield meaningful results than would quantitative research. Therefore, the survey responses I present here are intended to provide additional ethnographic illustration. They are not intended as data for the purpose of hypothesis testing.

Discussion

Certain aspects of this study may be idiosyncratic to South Haven, particularly those issues that relate to the program's admissions policies and curriculum. For example, South Haven students are not allowed to take courses outside the college during their first year, a higher level of segregation than is found in many other developmental programs. This segregation may increase the students' sense of difference and stigmatization.

The ethnographic monologues provide further clues into the meaning of the students' statements concerning stigma. The high school designation is repeatedly applied throughout the students' interview transcripts, as they draw binary distinctions between South Haven and the rest of the university. The following qualities were noted as evidence that South Haven is like high school: easy courses, small classes, all classes in the same building, lack of course options, no major, attendance policies, and high levels of oversight by advisors and teachers. Conversely, in constructing their view of the real college, students assumed that students in other university colleges classes experienced a greater range of course options, more difficult courses, larger classes, no attendance policies, little authoritative oversight, and great personal autonomy, in general.

For our students, South Haven High looks and feels like a high school in the middle of a real college. This presents South Haven faculty and administration with a dilemma. The same attributes that allow South Haven to succeed in its mission may sometimes cause resentment among students. The presence of a single building, for example, allows faculty, staff, supplemental instructors, advisors, and administrators to function as an integrated whole. Likewise, having a separate building and separate college allows the program to maintain greater stability and continuity than it would if subsumed within another college and spread across campus. Yet, for some students, the building is symbolic of high school, and, therefore, the program is experienced as an extended adolescent learning experience. Therefore, the most commonly used derogatory term for the program refers directly to the building in which the program is housed, which I will call Emerson Hall. Students often refer to South Haven as "Emerson High."

In support of their claim, several students mentioned the presence of student cohorts hanging out smoking together on the steps "just like in high school." The fact that they get to know each other well and take many classes together reminds students more of life in high school than college. By college they mean large public universities, like the larger institution to which South Haven belongs, not small liberal arts institutions. South Haven students see this as an indicator that they are not yet considered ready for full entrance into the university community.

Similarly, other potentially positive attributes are negatively perceived when filtered through the students' college versus high school binary. Small classes allow for better teaching, but also lead students to believe they are missing out on the real college, which has large lecture classes. In fact, several students cited small classes as a positive aspect of their South Haven education, and practically in the next breath used class size as evidence that South Haven is more like high school than real college.

Lisle Carter (1978) argues, "the best chances for" the success of students who have been traditionally excluded from higher education "are to be found in small residential programs" (p.97). Yet, large two and four-year urban institutions "are expected to bear the principal burden in assuming equality of opportunity for higher education" (p.97). South Haven, although hardly a small residential college, has taken admirable steps toward providing the sort of integrated education, including small classes, that helps students to succeed. Thus, the graduation rate five years after transfer for South Haven students who transfer to the university's College of Liberal Arts (CLA) is roughly equal to the five-year graduation rate for students initially admitted to CLA. Yet, it would appear that this success often comes at the cost of student resentment and feelings of stigmatization while they are enrolled at South Haven.

Attending small classes, seeing the same people in different classes, being segregated from the rest of the university, being looked at as "different"—these were precisely the qualities that students liked about the academically elite program where I taught during the previous four years. As high-achieving students admitted to an innovative School of Interdisciplinary Studies program, their sense of segregation is experienced in positive terms. Students outside the program see them as weird, creative, nonconformist, and smart. In the retro parlance of the day, they are viewed as "hippies." They wear this potential stigma as a badge of distinction. Conversely, the last thing developmental students want to be seen as is different. Even potential benefits, like smaller classes, are viewed as stigmata, symbolic of the difference between their own experience and students' lives in the real college.

As for easy classes, one wonders what South Haven students are using as a basis for comparison. Most of them have never experienced other college classes. Furthermore, South Haven students do very well, on average, after transferring into other colleges, assuming they do well enough to transfer in the first place. Conversely, students from other colleges do not necessarily perform at higher levels than their South Haven peers. In fact, non-South Haven students often perform relatively poorly in our courses. These students fall prey to the mistaken claim that our classes are much easier than those in their home colleges. A semester in South Haven classes usually corrects that notion. There is nothing to challenge such beliefs for South Haven students, however, because they are not allowed to take courses outside of South Haven during their first year.

Students may be mistaking "better" for "easier." I am not claiming the level of instruction at South Haven is necessarily superior to other colleges within the university. However, the smaller class sizes, focus on student development, and learning support may help students to perform better and learn more. Thus, it may seem South Haven courses are easier than those without such structural advantages and teaching supports. Then again, maybe some of the classes simply are easier. It is nearly impossible to determine whether or not this perception is accurate. Regardless, it must be taken seriously.

Whether accurate or not, negative associations and feelings of stigma persist. Even though student informants expressed many positive views about their actual educational experiences in South Haven, they also express a sense of stigmatization and embarrassment as South Haven students. Interview results would seem to indicate that much of their sense of stigmatization has to do with their relative segregation as learners within the university, the small size of South Haven relative to the other colleges, and other aspects of the program that mark it and its students as different from the rest of the university. Because many of these negatively defined aspects also represent distinct learning advantages, it is hard to imagine a simple way out of this conundrum.

Social Theory and Stigma

Perhaps the students' sense of stigma can be better understood when placed in larger social and theoretical contexts. Although social theory often falls flat when trying to develop practical solutions in the classroom, it is useful to occasionally step back and think about the larger social processes that condition our teaching and learning. I recognize that I am taking a leap from limited micro-experience as a developmental educator to broad macro-theory concerning the place of developmental education in the larger social world. In fact, one reviewer of this chapter referred to the following as "bombastic and vitriolic." Therefore, let me repeat that I am presenting this analysis as a set of theoretical possibilities, questions, and contexts, rather than laying claim to a definitive truth.

Every stratified social system produces stigma. To function, systems of extreme social inequality require ideological legitimation, including cultural narratives and ritual practices that make social inequality seem natural, rather than socially constructed (Althusser, 1972; Gramsci & Buttigieg, 1992). In the case of the U.S. academic system, ideological legitimation takes place partly through rituals of testing and grade ranking. These rituals focus attention on the individual student, so that achievement appears to be solely the result of internal, individual qualities rather than social structures. This extreme and exclusive focus on individuals diverts attention from the many social, political, economic, and cultural factors that condition academic performance, particularly at the population level (Kozol, 1991). Therefore, as a result of the testing and ranking ritual, the success of the mainly White, upper class populations who occupy elite educational strata appears to be the outcome of individual achievement alone, rather than the result of social privilege. This individuated focus allows those in administrative and legislative positions to ignore questions concerning the inequitable distribution of educational resources, sociolinguistic bias toward "standard" or "White" English, racism, sexism, and myriad other social factors.

In other words, grading and testing rituals legitimate academic inequality by placing our focus on individual student performance alone. The testing-ranking system thus obscures the social processes that lead entire populations to succeed academically while others largely fail. In addition to sanctioning the performance of individuals, therefore, the testing-ranking system legitimates a much larger system of privilege and deprivation. Stigma is the inevitable by-product of that ideological, individuating process. If you are not succeeding academically, there is something lacking inside you as an individual. Therefore, you are assumedly in need of "remediation" or "development." Although individual factors should certainly not be ignored (I could certainly use both remediation and development in certain academic areas of study), neither should these larger social realities that condition individual and group success.

The United States is a metropole (i.e., political and economic center) in one of the most extreme systems of social inequality the world has ever known. Therefore, we cannot speak solely of the United States' social system if we are to capture an accurate sense of contemporary social existence, because we live in an age of global economic integration and inequality. Witness the difference between the 589 million dollar annual income of Disney Chief Executive Office Michael Eisner and that of his assembly workers throughout the world, most of whom make less than $10,000 a year (i.e., the same amount he earns every two minutes). Such extremes are typical today between those at the top and those working for them throughout the world. In between is a middle class that enjoys some of the privileges of that exploitative system (e.g., inordinately cheap goods), while paying some of its costs (e.g., managerial labor and stress). One cannot speak of education as if it is somehow outside of this fundamental system of social organization. Globalization is redirecting who receives what sort of education, and where. Inner city students are increasingly trained to fill service roles, as the United States and other dominant nations are transforming into information and service-based economies, while Mexico and other Third

World countries are transformed into bases for manufacturing. Meanwhile, elite academic curricula in the United States are being internationalized in the interest of creating a more effective transnational managerial class.

Even if one chooses to look solely at the United States, we can still speak of extreme inequality. Jack Beatty's (1999) *Against Inequality* presents a basic statistical outline of income inequality provides links to several longer studies of socioeconomic inequality in the contemporary United States. Yet, despite the reality of extreme inequality, an ideology of individual opportunity prevails in the United States. The Horatio Alger, or perhaps, "Sam Walton" tales of successful, upwardly mobile individuals ideologically replace more accurate understandings of class inequality and corporate power. Sociological imagination (Mills, 1959) is replaced by the myth of individual opportunity. Thus, in the United States, if you have not attained a higher position than that into which you were born, you have failed to develop successfully, academically and otherwise. You have not passed the test.

In the United States the racial-caste and economic-class systems are inextricably linked, influencing virtually everything we do as social agents. Therefore, it would stand to reason that developmental programs like South Haven would become natural targets of the stigmatization process. After all, South Haven and similar programs elsewhere are populated with racially and ethnically diverse student bodies, inordinate numbers of working-class students, and a group of students marked as educational failures. Thus, our students' feelings of stigma should not take us by surprise. Yet, in my case it did. As long as we function within a system of extreme social inequality—and as long as education remains central to this ideological process—there will be an academic elite and an academic underclass. Therefore, whether we call them remedial, special, developmental, or any other word we contrive, our students will be attributed, and feel, a sense of educational stigma.

Much of the battle appears to be over how willing the academic elite will be to allow an academic underclass to penetrate their own borders, rather than remain safely segregated in community colleges. Carter (1978) reminds us that two-year institutions have too often "been used by the four-year institution to avoid its responsibilities" (p.97). In that light, the move to defund developmental education programs represents nothing less than an attempt at ritual purification, betraying a deeply held belief that developmental programs and students do not truly belong. Our presence is polluting.

In other words, I do not believe that the stigma expressed by South Haven students can be explained solely in terms of individual feelings of failure, or even systemic dysfunction. Our students are alienated by design. Rather than the result of an otherwise good system that occasionally fails, our students and their stigma are products of a bad system which functions all too well, ideologically and otherwise, to maintain a system of power and privilege. After all, how could a hierarchical system rationalize the inordinate privilege of its academic (and financial) elite without also stigmatizing those on the bottom of that hierarchy?

Recommendations

Although, in retrospect, it seems natural that students in a developmental education program would feel a sense of social stigma, I was totally unprepared for it as a teacher. I am only now beginning to develop ways to deal with the students' feelings of alienation. I start by explaining to students that the readings, exercises, and lectures I use at South Haven are basically the same I have used in supposedly elite college contexts. I remind them that small classes are not a punishment but rather a positive aspect of South Haven, akin to a small liberal arts college. Such disclosures seem to have some positive effects.

How we present ourselves is key, as is the way we represent our students. Jeanne Higbee (2000) reminds us that developmental educators "must pay attention to how we describe the students we serve." (p.) Indeed, semantics are important. Language that emphasizes student deficits relative to university standards is potentially debilitating for students. When described in remedial terms, our students appear to simply be below average, rather than students with individual skills, interests, and needs. Personally, I like teaching students who have more than merely scholastic aims and interests, and I have not found real or perceived academic deficits to be the defining features of my students. Plus, in addition to these issues of internal representation, remedial language places developmental programs in danger of falling under the budget axe externally (Garnett & Hood, 1998). Developmental theory is, therefore, a major advance over the remedial terminology and mindset.

Yet, even the term developmental remains problematic. It is what anthropologists refer to as an etic category (Harris, 1968, p. 571) (i.e., defined by the researcher or other cultural outsider) rather than a term students themselves would choose to apply (i.e., the emic category (Harris, 1968, p. 571)). Not one student I have queried in South Haven has heard of "developmental education." This is evidence that our students have remained the objects of our learning project, rather than actively enfranchised subjects in the Freirian (1993) tradition. We should not only modify our language, therefore, but also let students collaborate in the educational process. To that end, I propose that we consider incorporating a justice model into developmental education.

The Educational Justice Model

That last point brings me to what I see as a complementary model for developmental education: educational justice. A justice model requires that we become more aware of the social contexts that condition our teaching praxis. A focus on justice demands that we not only assist individual students in their development, but also attempt to transform the system that produces and devalues them.

I recognize that regardless of what model we adopt, there will always be a conundrum involved in working with students whose test scores and grades place them in developmental programs. If we openly acknowledge the inevitable remedial function of such programs, there is the danger of heightening the students' sense of stigma. If we merely change the language to fit a more positive framework, we run the risk of academic pretense. The history of the term "special" within educational settings serves as a warning to all who would wish away the realities of our work through the alchemy of linguistic code switching alone. Whether we call our practice remedial or developmental education the field will fail to become the transformative social force many would like it to be if we do not also engage in a critical debate concerning the larger social goals and contexts of developmental education.

Likewise, the justice model is fraught with conundrums and contradictions. First, as is already true in developmental education, the gravitational pull of remedialism would be difficult to overcome, both in word and deed, even if such a model were adopted. We will still need to help students gain reading, writing, math, and thinking skills that will allow them to succeed academically. We can only hope that they will become agents of transformation in the process, using both their prior and newfound skills to remake the educational system.

Second, there would likely be a severe contradiction between student and faculty orientations if we began to more openly promote a justice model. The great majority of student informants interviewed in the South Haven study noted a strong desire to simply slip in and out of the program without undo attention to their having been enrolled in South Haven. As one student-informant explained: "I feel that most South Haven students are about the same; we all want to get out of South Haven and into different colleges." Of the 125 students surveyed by Valeri-Gold and her colleagues (1997), 25 expressed a similar desire to "exit developmental studies classes as soon as possible." A number of the students in that study found developmental classes "a waste of time and an embarrassment" (p. 7).

As opposed to the current developmental model, however, the justice model asks students to consciously reflect upon the larger social processes that have conditioned their academic lives. The testimonials of Rigoberta Menchu (Menchu & Burgos-Debray, 1984), Elvia Alvarado (Alvardo, Benjamin, & Institute for Food and Development Policy, 1987), and others who have taken part in Freirian (1993) education demonstrate the practical educational benefits of such reflection. Sociological imagination allows one to not only gain the skills necessary to succeed, but also to reflect upon the larger social factors that have conditioned past failure. Through such critical reflection, students can begin to recognize that they are not alone, and that many others like them have been setup to fail within a system predicated on differential success and failure, privilege and oppression. However, most U.S. students would prefer to simply get the goods and get out. They would prefer to reduce their sense of stigma rather than openly reflect upon it and fight it. Therefore, many students react angrily to a justice-oriented pedagogy.

In a society that tends to mark the beneficiaries of justice as inferior, students may not want us to emphasize the social justice aspects of developmental education. Note the stigma surrounding those admitted to universities via affirmative action (Turner & Pratkanis, 1996). Many students would rather get help with the academic skills they need in order to succeed, and then move on as soon as possible, rather than be viewed as the recipients of justice along the way. Furthermore, there is potential for such practices to be viewed as liberal noblesse oblige, rather than as a movement for educational equality and justice.

Despite these difficulties and dangers, the justice model could be an important complement to the developmental paradigm. Developmental programs should be at the heart of the attempt to make public universities live up to their most important standard: public education. Perhaps if we advance the justice argument, we could be viewed as central to the academic mission, rather than ephemeral support for individual students who, for whatever reasons, appear to lag behind in their development.

Unfortunately, it would seem that developmental education programs prefer to downplay the social justice aspect of their mission. I have seen little explicit attention to justice and injustice in the official discourse of developmental education programs, and have seen little attention to questions of educational justice at the NADE and College Reading and Learning Association (CRLA) conferences. Such organizations and conferences do exist—for example, the annual Pedagogy and Theatre of the Oppressed Conference. However, the field of developmental education itself seems to maintain a small-scale theoretical focus, based almost exclusively on theories derived from the discipline of developmental psychology. While such theories are fundamental, I think that we must also expand the field to include research and theory concerning the larger cultural and political economic contexts within which we teach and learn.

Although it may seem like pragmatism to emphasize individual development and downplay social justice, might it not be counter-productive? Lacking a strong argument for our presence, and the presence of our students in a selective research-oriented institution, we wear a permanent "kick me" sign on our backs, just waiting for the budget boot to arrive once the state economy turns sour, again. In other words, we may actually invite academic stigma through our failure to actively, effectively, and continually argue that students from lower income families and other marginalized social groups have a rightful place in the university, even if they have not successfully performed in the testing and grade-ranking rituals. It is not a matter of individual development alone, but also a matter of social justice.

Classroom Practices: Enfranchising Students

Leaving larger scale questions and returning to the classroom, there are promising methods for dealing with issues of stigma in our teaching. Although difficult conundrums and contradictions are inevitable by-products of important work, there may be a few ways to work through them, starting with classroom teaching practices based on collective learning and critical analysis, rather than individual development alone.

First, I would suggest enfranchising students by honestly communicating our central goals and reason for being. This should not be left to orientation counselors and advisors alone. We, as instructors, must continue the process of communication and reflection concerning why students are in our classrooms, what our stake is in their education, and what their role is in our research.

No matter how we frame it, the most immediate goal in programs like South Haven is to augment the skills and knowledge base of students who, for whatever reasons, have not gained the necessary skills and qualifications for admission into the larger university. If there is a major remedial component, perhaps we should openly recognize this. Second, as noted by Higbee (2000), we should emphasize the more universal, developmental aspects of our educational practices, so that our students may feel less isolated and alienated while going through the process of learning those necessary skills.

Finally, and perhaps most importantly, I suggest that we openly acknowledge and attempt to transform the contexts of power within which we work. Rather than simply waiting for drowning victims to come floating by, we should also occasionally wade upstream to find out what is causing so many boats to capsize. This step, more than any other, requires that we enfranchise our students in the educational process, perhaps starting by letting them in on the fact that they are part of this thing called developmental education. Rather than treat students solely as learners in need of development, we must also engage them in a learning process that seeks more than individual advancement up the social ladder.

The collaborative ethnographic study this article is based on, although not designed with the above goals in mind, seems to have integrated those learning objectives fairly well. Students became active researchers and informants, rather than mere research subjects, or objects. Students were also able to use their research experience in order to reflect upon the nature of the institution and, hopefully, it will help them to navigate more effectively through it. The research project also provided a safe space for students to talk about their South Haven experience. It was not always a pleasant experience, but as illustrated in Laurence Simon's (1998) provocative argument, *Psychology, Education, Gods, and Humanity*, critical reflection concerning the educational process is often the best way to teach "students who would rather be elsewhere" (p.158).

Conclusions

Many South Haven students feel a sense of stigma. I suspect that South Haven is not unique in that regard. Yet, there is very little written about the topic in the developmental education literature. Perhaps this silence is caused by faculty reticence to discuss the potentially negative aspects of developmental education, fearing that it may serve to weaken external support for our programs. I disagree. I believe it is crucial that we make the discussion of stigma and other important cultural realities part of our research and teaching agenda. How can we hope to positively transform our institutions if we do not fully explore the students' experience within them and attitudes toward them?

Beyond fear of reprisal, there may be more immediate reasons why developmental educators have chosen to avoid the issue of stigma. The stigma of remedial education falls not only upon our students, but upon us as well. Just as our students often feel like second class citizens, so too, we all feel at least somewhat marginalized relative to the faculty who teach in disciplinary departments. If we explore the culture of stigma completely, we will find that such feelings color much of what we do as teachers and learners. Like many of our students, however, we rarely choose to openly engage and express such feelings. Perhaps that is one of the reasons why we are more comfortable treating our students as research subjects than in becoming part of the research gaze ourselves. Yet, despite our best objectivist attempts to distance ourselves from our subject(s), it is not hard to find, mirrored in the unpublished background of every article and book concerning who they are as students, a set of questions concerning who and what we are as developmental educators.

I would argue, however, that we have nothing to fear. In fact, the best way to combat stigmatization may be to make our conversation about stigma more of an overt element of our teaching and research practice. This may move us beyond issues of individual deficits and development alone and toward a model of educational justice in the tradition of Sor Juana Ines de la Cruz (1997), Dewey (1966), Freire (1993), and other developmental educators who emphasize justice rather than deficits, and whose pedagogy places individual academic development in the wider context of collective social development.

Currently, however, the dominant model in developmental education appears to be that of enculturation. Many developmental educators see their sole and primary mission as that of helping individual students gain the skills they need in order to operate and succeed within the social hierarchy. Although I see that as an inevitable outcome of our teaching, it is an incomplete model and a losing proposition. To the extent that we fail to challenge the educational hierarchy, we serve to reproduce it and the stigma it generates.

Therefore, in addition to helping the system work for a select few, we must also advocate for the majority who do not have access to quality postsecondary education. We should subvert the easy sophistries upon which elite education is predicated by emphasizing social, as well as individual, development. Whether we call such an orientation the pedagogy of the oppressed, justice education, participatory education, or democratic education, such a conception will move us closer to fulfilling the promises of public education. Although an orientation toward justice education may not remove the stigma attached to developmental education programs, students, and faculty, it may allow us to develop new ways to challenge the system that produces it.

References

Althusser, L. (1972). *Lenin and philosophy, and other essays*. New York: Monthly Review.

Alvarado, E., Benjamin, M., & Institute for Food and Development Policy (Oakland, CA). (1987). *Don't be afraid, gringo: A Honduran woman speaks from the heart: The story of Elvia Alvarado*. San Francisco: Institute for Food and Development Policy.

Beatty, J. (1999, April). *Against inequality* [Online]. Available: http://www.theatlantic.com/issues/99apr/9904inequality.htm

Brown, L. (1998). Ethnic stigma as a contextual experience: A possible selves perspective. *Personality and Social Psychology Bulletin, 24*(2), 163-172.

Carter, L.C., Jr. (1978). What standard for equal opportunity? In J.W. Peltason & M.V. Massengale (Eds.), *Students and their institutions: A changing relationship* (pp. 94-99). Washington, DC: American Council on Education.

Castro, B. (1974). Hostos: Report from a ghetto college. *Harvard Educational Review, 44*(2), 270-294.

Dewey, J. (1966). *Democracy and education: An introduction to the philosophy of education* (Free Press paperback edition. ed.). New York: Free Press.

Dougherty, S., Campana, K., Kontos, R., Flores, M., Lockhart, R., & Shaw, D. (1996). Supported education: A qualitative study of the student experience. *Psychiatric Rehabilitation Journal, 19*(3), 59-70.

Freire, P. (1993). *Pedagogy of the oppressed* (New rev. 20th-anniversary ed.). New York: Continuum.

Garnett, D.T., & Hood, M.V., III. (1998). Provisionally admitted college students: Do they belong in a research university? In J.L. Higbee & P.L. Dwinell (Eds.), *Developmental education: Preparing successful college students* (pp. 49-54). Columbia, SC: National Resource Center for The First-Year Experience and Students in Transition, University of South Carolina.

Gilbert, D. (1998). The Prejudice Perception Assessment Scale: Measuring stigma vulnerability among African-American students at predominantly Euro-American universities. *Journal of Black Psychology, 24*(3), 305-21.

Gramsci, A., & Buttigieg, J.A. (1992). *Prison notebooks.* New York: Columbia University.

Hardin, C.J. (1998). Who belongs in college: A second look. In J.L. Higbee & P.L. Dwinell (Eds.), *Developmental education: Preparing successful college students* (pp. 15-24). Columbia, SC: National Resource Center for The First-Year Experience and Students in Transition, University of South Carolina.

Harris, M. (1968). *The rise of anthropological theory.* New York: Harper & Row.

Higbee, J. (2000). Who is the developmental student? *The Learning Assistance Review, 5*(1), 41-50.

Inés de la Cruz, J., Peden, M.S., & Stavans, I. (1997). *Poems, protest, and a dream: Selected writings.* New York: Penguin.

Kamwamgamalu, N. (1997). Multilingualism and education policy in post-apartheid South Africa. *Language Problems and Language Planning, 21*(3), 234-253.

Kozol, J. (1991). *Savage inequalities: Children in America's schools* (1st ed.). New York: Crown.

Low, J. (1996). Negotiating identities, negotiating environments: An interpretation of the experiences of students with disabilities. *Disability & Society, 11*(2), 235-248.

MacDonald, R.B. (1987). *Evaluation of an alternative solution for the assessment and retention of high-risk college students.* Paper presented at the Annual Meeting of the American Educational Research Association, Washington D.C.

Menchú, R., & Burgos-Debray, E. (1984). *I, Rigoberta Menchú: An Indian woman in Guatemala.* London: Verso.

Miller, S., & Evko, B. (1985). An ethnographic study of the influence of a mobile home community on suburban high school students. *Human Relations, 38*(7), 683-705.

Mills, C. (1959). *The sociological imagination.* New York: Oxford University.

Northcraft, G. B. (1983). *The stigma of affirmative action: An empirical analysis.* Paper presented at the Annual Convention of the Rocky Mountain Psychological Association, Snowbird, Utah.

Pedelty, M. (1995). *War stories: The culture of foreign correspondents.* New York: Routledge.

Royster, V. (1983). Watching the pendulum in education. *American Scholar, 5*(2), 193-204.

Schafer, W., Olexa, C., & Polk, K. (1970). Programmed for social class: Tracking in high school. *Trans-Action, 7*(12), 39-46, 63.

Simon, L.R. (1998). *Psychology, education, gods, and humanity.* Westport, CN: Praeger.

Smith, A.D. (1993). *Fires in the mirror: Crown Heights, Brooklyn, and other identities* (1st Anchor Books ed.). New York: Anchor Books/Doubleday.

Smith, G. (1998). The ideology of "fag": The school experience of gay students. *The Sociological Quarterly, 39*(2), 309-305.

Turner, M.E., & Pratkanis, A. (1996). The proactive removal of discriminatory barriers: Affirmative action as effective help. *Journal of Social Issues, 52*(4), 111-132.

Valeri-Gold, M., Callahan, C.A., Deming, M.P., Mangram, M.T., & Errico, M. (1997). Reflections: Experience commentaries by urban developmental studies students. In P.L. Dwinell & J.L. Higbee (Eds.), *Developmental education: Enhancing student retention* (pp. 3-18). Carol Stream, IL: National Association for Developmental Education.

Wiltfang, G., & Scarbecz, M. (1990). Social class and adolescents' self-esteem: Another look. *Social Psychology Quarterly, 53*(2), 174-183.

Developmental Education and Alfred Binet: The Original Purpose of Standardized Testing

Patrick R. Perdew

Austin Peay State University

Abstract

Alfred Binet invented mental tests to determine whether an individual had a need for remedial or developmental education. Tracing the history of such testing reveals, however, that his successors utilized the tests for other purposes. Reviewing literature concerning the use and misuse of testing in America during the twentieth century shows how the tests became associated with the hereditarian theory of intelligence, eugenics, immigration restrictions, meritocracy, race, and affirmative action. The Scholastic Aptitude Test, and the newly developed Strivers score, are also discussed. Collegiate developmental education programs continue to use tests in the way Binet envisioned when he invented them nearly 100 years ago.

Mental testing began in France with Alfred Binet in the early 1900s. Its original purpose was to determine need for remediation, prior to the conceptualization of developmental education. Soon thereafter, however, when mental tests were brought to America, they became tied to the eugenics movement through the hereditarian view of intelligence. Eugenics advocated improving genetic stock through controlled reproduction (Gould, 1998). Hereditarians believed intelligence was determined entirely by genetic factors and

For further information contact: Patrick R. Perdew • Austin Peay State University • P. O. Box 4476 • Clarksville, TN 37044 • e-mail: perdewp@apsu.edu could not be improved significantly through environmental changes (Gould, 1998). At the beginning of a new century, it seems appropriate to reflect upon the uses, and abuses, of standardized testing. Developmental educators still utilize the tests in the sense that Binet intended: to assess need of remedial or developmental instruction. However, some misuses of aptitude tests can still occur through the philosophy of meritocracy, if the background and experience of the test taker is not taken into consideration during admissions decisions. The Strivers project, an adjustment of Scholastic Aptitude Test (SAT) scores by the Educational Testing Service, takes such background factors into consideration (Glazer & Thernstrom, 1999).

Origins of Standardized Testing

Alfred Binet

In 1904 the Minister of Public Education in France commissioned Alfred Binet to identify children whose academic difficulties indicated need for special education (Gould, 1995). So the French psychologist devised a set of tasks to assess a student's reasoning potential with a single score. After assigning age levels to the tasks in 1908, Binet called the score obtained "mental age" (Gould, 1981). If the mental age was significantly below a student's chronological age, then a need for remediation was indicated.

In public schools in France at that time, classes were large and the curriculum was rigid; teachers had no time to devote to students with special needs (Gould, 1995). Binet advocated special classrooms and instruction programs for students needing remediation as shown by his test. His suggestions included small class size (i.e., 15 to 20 students) and study skills instruction (Gould, 1981), strategies still utilized by developmental programs today. Binet's remedial programs were successful. In a 1909 paper he stated, "the intelligence of these students has been increased. We have increased what constitutes the intelligence of a pupil: the capacity to learn and assimilate instruction" (as cited in Gould, 1995, p. 18).

Later, in 1912, the German psychologist William Stern defined "intelligence quotient" or IQ as the ratio of mental age to chronological age multiplied by 100 (Gould, 1981). Binet, however, always maintained that intelligence was too complex a biological property to be expressed as a single number. In 1905 he wrote "the scale, properly speaking, does not permit the measure of the intelligence because intellectual qualities are not superposable, and therefore cannot be measured as linear surfaces are measured" (as cited in Gould, 1995, p. 18). Binet feared his scale could be misused if extended to the general population and the scores used as a label rather than a means to identify students requiring help (Gould, 1981; Owen, 1985). Unfortunately, what he had feared soon took place in America. However, Binet (1857 - 1911) could not protest, an untimely death having stilled his voice.

Henry H. Goddard

Henry H. Goddard, a psychologist, translated Binet's work into English in 1910 (Owen, 1985). He tested 2000 students in the public schools of Vineland, New Jersey and found several he believed to be mentally deficient (Goodenough, 1949). However, his translation of Binet's test was incorrect and caused harsh scoring (Gould, 1981). Far from observing Binet's caveat regarding labels, Goddard invented one for a person with a mental age between 8 and 12: moron (Gould, 1981). He advocated general use of IQ tests and, being a eugenicist, believed that no "feeble-minded" (i.e., IQ < 70) person should be allowed to reproduce (Gould, 1981).

The eugenics movement was "the early twentieth century's most influential social crusade with an allegedly scientific foundation" (Gould, 1998, p. 25). Mendel's laws of genetics had been rediscovered and published in 1900 (Gould, 1998). The Mendelian principles were being misused, however, when geneticists tried to link single genes to complex human characteristics such as intelligence. Eugenics espoused improvement of genetic stock. Negative eugenics sought to prevent reproduction of those alleged to be inferior, and positive eugenics encouraged reproduction of those alleged to be superior (Gould, 1998). This movement led to immigration restrictions and was associated with the hereditarian view of intelligence.

Goddard stated that morons, as he had labeled them, should not have children (as cited in Gould, 1981). In 1912 Goddard claimed (as cited in Goodenough, 1949) that mental deficiency tended to run in families and was linked to immorality, delinquency, and crime, popular views of eugenicists. Committing an egregious error, if not outright falsehood, Rudolph Pintner, a mental test author at the time, wrote in 1922 that the reason for the development of the Binet scale was "the need of society to protect itself against the feeble-minded" (p. 153). The original intentions of Alfred Binet were being perverted by eugenicists. He had developed mental testing as a method of identifying students demonstrating a need for special education so their potential could be enhanced, and later they could be integrated into regular classroom settings. In direct opposition, eugenicists thought persons with low IQs should not reproduce and should be excluded from society. Furthermore, hereditarians believed no educational amelioration was possible.

Goddard and others were basing their arguments upon hereditarianism, a fallacious theory of biological determinism: This view asserted that a certain behavior is determined solely by genetic makeup and cannot be changed significantly by environmental factors (Gould, 1998). In a 1914 paper (as cited in Gould, 1981) Goddard stated, with no supporting evidence, that mental deficiency was governed by a single gene. Although some attributes have an innate basis and a deterministic view is legitimate, this is not the case with intelligence. It is also true that genetic endowment influences behavior, but it does not set inevitable bounds on intelligence. Biology and environment combine to produce intelligence, and all other complex characteristics and behaviors, and the interaction is not adversarial as "nature versus nurture" seems to imply. Education is not an assault upon inborn biological limits (Gould, 1995). According to Gould (1995), the greatest tragedy of biological determinism occurs if, accepting the premise of immutable limits, "we give up . . ., but could have helped, then we have committed the most grievous error of chaining the human spirit" (p. 19). Far from giving up, today's developmental educators are providing a beneficial learning experience some students have not encountered in previous school environments.

Henry H. Goddard later realized he was in error. In 1914 he had written "every feeble-minded person is a potential criminal" (as cited in Freeman, 1926, p. 427), but in 1924 Murchison (as cited in Freeman) tested several thousand convicts, finding only a slight relation to intelligence in case of assault-type crimes, while the majority of criminals committing fraud were actually of superior intelligence. In 1928, Goddard (as cited in Gould, 1981) recanted the views he had earlier espoused as a hereditarian and eugenicist. He lowered the upper limit for feeble-mindedness on his test and stated that morons (again, Goddard's term) were not incurable and should not be segregated. Instead, supporting Binet, Goddard argued that morons should be educated and trained.

Lewis M. Terman

Goddard's translation of Binet was widely used in the U. S. until the Stanford Revision of the Binet scale by Lewis M. Terman was published in 1916 (Freeman, 1926). Terman was a professor at Stanford University and his scale, known as the Stanford-Binet IQ test, became the standard for testing in the U. S. (Goodenough, 1949). Terman introduced IQ or intelligence quotient in America; Goddard's translation used Binet's concept of mental age (Goodenough). Despite these revisions of Binet's scale, and others later by Terman in 1937 and 1960, the content of the Stanford-Binet can mostly be traced back to the original by Binet (Carroll, 1982).

Terman was a hereditarian, stating in 1906 that endowment was of greater importance than training in determining intelligence (as cited in Gould, 1981). Terman was also a eugenicist. In 1916, Terman wrote that a feeble-minded person would not be an efficient worker nor a responsible citizen, and did not wish them to reproduce (as cited in Gould, 1981). Terman added (as cited in Gould, 1981) that there were racial differences in intelligence that were due to genetic endowment rather than environment. However, as Gould (1981) pointed out, this false hereditarian viewpoint did not consider the impoverished conditions of the Hispanics in the southwest, Native Americans on reservations, and African Americans in the segregated South, who were included in the population tested. In 1937, Terman realized the falseness of the hereditarian theory of intelligence and recanted his earlier views, stating that differences between groups were due to environment and that mean differences between social classes were too small to make predictions about individuals (as cited in Gould, 1981). By doing this, he earned the dedication in Goodenough's (1949) book on mental testing: "To Lewis M. Terman — A Worthy Successor to Alfred Binet" (p. v).

Race, Ethnicity, and Testing

Cultural Differences

Terman was not the first to use faulty reasoning to allege racial differences in intelligence. Nor, unfortunately, would he be the last. Joseph-Arthur Gobineau (1816-1882) was "the grandfather of modern academic racism" (Gould, 1995, p. 12). He stated that there was a universal belief in "innate and permanent differences in the moral and mental endowments of the various groups of the human species" (as cited in Gould, 1995, p.12). His work inspired a social movement known as Gobinism (Gould, 1995), a precursor to the eugenics movement in America in the next century. Also, through Houston Stewart Chamberlain, Gobineau's ideas formed the foundation of racial theories supported by Hitler (Gould, 1995). Seeking mathematical evidence for his racist claims, Gobineau turned to craniometry (i.e., skull measurement) and other such methods (Gould, 1995). These techniques were, of course, completely invalid. Alfred Binet demonstrated in 1900 that craniometry did not measure intelligence (as cited in Gould, 1981).

After their development by Binet, mental tests were then misused by others to form the basis of most claims about human inequality (Gould, 1995). In fact, Gould (1995) defines the hereditarian theory of IQ as "the imposition of Binet's apparatus upon Gobineau's argument" (p. 17). Though false, the hereditarian theory has resurfaced at different times in discussions of race and IQ. In 1973, Jensen (as cited in Scarr & Carter-Saltzmann, 1982) said IQ differences between Blacks and Whites were primarily due to genetic factors, but four other studies during the 1970s (as cited in Scarr & Carter-Saltzmann) rejected that conclusion and cited cultural factors. Another revival of the hereditarian view occurred more recently. In an essay critical of *The Bell Curve* by Herrnstein and Murray (1994), Stephen J. Gould wrote "the form of argument about average intelligence among racial groups is no different and no more supportable than Gobineau's founding version" (1995, p. 17).

As early as the 1920s, cultural factors were listed, along with other environmental aspects such as economic and educational background, as a reason for IQ differences. Cultural theorists argued that tests involved questions and reflected a concept of intelligence that were culture-dependent (Laboratory of Comparative Human Cognition, 1982). For this reason, and because people of diverse genotypes cannot be randomized over environment in order to get a sample from which inferences could be drawn about a population, several scientists doubt that well-designed research about the genetic role in intelligence is even possible (Scarr & Carter-Saltzmann, 1982). Before this enlightenment about cultural and socioeconomic factors became widely accepted, there was another misapplication of mental tests concerning immigrants to the United States.

Army Mental Tests

Robert M. Yerkes, a psychologist at Harvard, along with Terman, Goddard, and others, created the Army Mental Tests during World War I (Owen, 1985). This marked the beginning of group testing with 1.75 million tested in 1917 (Gould, 1981). The Army tests were given to place draftees according to mentality (Freeman, 1926). Tests included the Army Alpha and Army Beta. The Alpha was a written test and the Beta was nonverbal (pictorial) for illiterate personnel or those who did not comprehend English (Carroll, 1982). Recruits with low scores then took Terman's Stanford-Binet IQ test (Freeman). Carl Campbell Brigham, a psychologist at Princeton whom Yerkes had met, analyzed the Army Mental Tests in 1923 in *A Study of American Intelligence* (Owen, 1985). Mental Age (MA) equivalents for the Army test scores were made using a selected group who took both the Alpha and Stanford-Binet (Freeman, 1926).

Freeman (1926) notes that significant race differences were found on Army Mental Tests when comparing Native Americans or African Americans and Whites. In 1923, Brigham (as cited in Owen, 1985) wrote of four racial strains in the U.S.: Nordic, Alpine, Mediterranean, and Negro. Eugenicists alleged that Nordics were superior (Freeman). However, there were also urban versus rural and North versus South differences, which ran against any racial hypothesis (Freeman). In fact, the average score of northern African Americans was higher than the average score of Whites in some southern states (Freeman). Freeman also noted that Massachusetts and Connecticut, which had a large proportion of non-Nordic immigrants, were near the top in state rankings. These findings ran counter to the views of both hereditarians and eugenicists that Nordics were superior. Freeman concluded that the score differences were due to educational and environmental differences, and that proponents of any hypothesis that alleged the superiority of Nordics had no support.

Immigration Restriction

Differences were also found among immigrants on the Army tests, with averages higher for those who had been in the U.S. longer (Freeman, 1926). This was because of test features on the Alpha that rewarded knowledge of American culture and language (Gould, 1981). For the most part, immigrants from eastern Europe arrived in the U.S. later than immigrants from western Europe, and this was reflected in the results. Men from Mexico, Italy, Portugal, Poland, and Greece scored lower on average than Jews, English, Swedes, Norwegians, and Germans (Goodenough, 1949). The fact that directions were given by pantomime on the non-language Beta (and, therefore, easily misunderstood) was another contributing factor for the lower scores of recent immigrants (Freeman). Thus, the scores of men of different nationalities reflected testing, environmental, and cultural factors.

Supporters of the eugenics movement, however, interpreted the scores of immigrants incorrectly using their hereditarian view. Brigham, in his aforementioned 1923 work about the tests, stated that Catholics, Jews, Negroes, Greeks, Hungarians, Italians, Poles, Russians, and Turks were innately less intelligent than people of western European descent (as cited in Owen, 1985). This false conclusion ignored the positive correlation between scores and years lived in America and, concerning Jews, did not agree with Goodenough's assessment mentioned above. As Freeman (1926) pointed out, comparing scores of immigrants who had been in the U.S. 15 to 20 years with scores of those here just a few years, as if their scores had the same significance, was erroneous. For further proof of Brigham's error, it is worth noting that Jews, as well as Asian Americans, score so high on the SAT today that they are overrepresented, in terms of their percentage of the population, at elite universities (Glazer & Thernstrom, 1999).

Brigham, being a hereditarian, believed the low scores meant a low unchangeable intelligence and indicated that some immigrant populations had little chance of success in America (Carroll, 1982). Furthermore, because he was a eugenicist as well, Brigham called for the halt of immigration in 1923 in order to prevent what he called "the propagation of defective strains in the present population" (as cited in Owen, 1985, p. 178). Though not substantiated, the wishes of the eugenicists were carried out when the Immigration Restriction Act was passed in

1924. This act set quotas that limited the number of immigrants. Gould (1981) stated that Brigham's 1923 interpretation of the Army Mental Test results in *A Study of American Intelligence* led to the 1924 restrictions.

Far from being used to uplift those in need, in accord with Binet's original wishes, intelligence tests were now being used to cast out the needy. During the 1930s, European Jews were denied visas when quotas were reached (Owen, 1985). The immigration laws were not relaxed so additional Jewish refugees could enter America, even when they sought to escape Hitler (Gould, 1998). "The New Colossus" (1883) by Emma Lazarus (as cited in Trachtenberg, 1976) on the pedestal of the Statue of Liberty concludes, "I lift my lamp beside the golden door!" (p. 214). Due in no small part to the eugenics movement and hereditarian theory of intelligence, many European Jews found this golden door shut when they needed to enter it most.

Carl Campbell Brigham later recanted, abandoning his hereditarian view and the eugenics movement. He stated, in the 1930 paper containing his recantation (as cited in Gould, 1981), that the Alpha and Beta tests could not be combined into one scale; the Beta test did not give measurements as accurate as the Alpha (Freeman, 1926). Brigham (as cited in Owen, 1985) also said there were errors in comparing Army Mental Test scores and Stanford-Binet test scores due to those comparisons being based on the scores of a select (i.e., unrepresentative) group of men, as mentioned earlier. Brigham concluded his 1930 article by stating that "comparative studies of various national and racial groups may not be made with existing tests" and "one of the most pretentious of these comparative racial studies — the writer's own — was without foundation" (as cited in Owen, p. 187).

After showing the racial tenets of eugenics (which, thankfully, faded out as a movement after World War II and the genocide practiced by Hitler) to be without justification, Brigham exposed the hereditarian view of intelligence as a fallacy as well. In a private memorandum, reported in 1961 by Downey, his biographer, Brigham wrote that the "testing movement came to America . . . accompanied by one of the most serious fallacies in the history of science, namely, that the tests measured native intelligence purely and simply without regard to training or schooling. I hope nobody believes that now" (as cited in Carroll, 1982, p. 63). The fallacy of hereditarianism that "accompanied" the testing movement into America was placed there by Goddard upon its arrival, and not by Binet upon its departure. Brigham further stated in the memorandum, "the test scores are a composite including schooling, family background, [and] familiarity with English" (as cited in Carroll, p. 63). Though the hereditarian view resurfaces briefly now and again (as in The Bell Curve), Brigham signaled its end as a widely-held scientific theory when he concluded the memo by announcing "the 'native intelligence' hypothesis is dead" (as cited in Carroll, p.63).

College Admissions and Testing

After the perceived "success" of the Army tests in World War I, a flood of similar ones followed (Carroll, 1982). There were between 4,000 and 5,000 mental tests by the late 1930s (Goodenough, 1949). The Army testing program also provided the impetus for testing in public schools (Miller, 1922). Miller warned that some of the tests were untried, and that school administrators were untrained in both giving and interpreting the tests. The Army's mass testing also influenced colleges to begin using intelligence tests for admission (Crouse & Trusheim, 1988). The Army Alpha was released for civilian use and adopted by colleges (Goodenough). In a summary of the use of intelligence tests in 29 colleges and universities, Whipple (1922) reported that the Army Alpha test was utilized in 16 of the institutions. The Army tests having been designed for males, Whipple stated the "Army Alpha test is so phrased and constituted as to favor men over women, though this objection is not particularly serious" (p. 254). His opinion in the last clause may have been predicated upon the relatively low collegiate enrollment of women at that time, but certainly would not be held by any woman denied admission because of a gender biased test. Even when some psychologists incorrectly held there were racial differences in intelligence, few ever stated there were gender differences. Freeman (1926) reviewed previous studies and concluded there were no significant gender differences in intellectual capacity, and also cited Terman's findings that girls scored slightly higher than boys up to age 13.

In 1919, Columbia University became the first institution to use an intelligence test, the Thorndike College Entrance Examination (Whipple, 1922), for admission (Crouse & Trusheim, 1988). Its president, Nicholas Murray Butler, advocated this in order to limit the enrollment of eastern European Jews and other first and second generation immigrants, which was increasing due to the university's proximity to New York City (Crouse & Trusheim). Immigrants were at a disadvantage because the tests involved knowledge of American culture. The elitist administrators held the view, expressed by eugenicists and hereditarians at that time, that a low score on the test reflected a student's innate intelligence (Carroll, 1982) and, therefore, used it to deny admission rather than to counsel or place the student. The fact that test scores correlated with students' demographic background was not taken into consideration (Carroll). This use of intelligence tests to exclude students was in direct opposition to Binet's purpose of inclusion when he invented them.

Scholastic Aptitude Test

The College Entrance Examination Board (CEEB) was established in 1900 (Crouse & Trusheim, 1988). In 1925, the College Board commissioned Carl Campbell Brigham to construct an admissions exam (Carroll, 1982). After World War I, Brigham had returned to Princeton, where he used the Army Alpha to test undergraduates (Owen, 1985). After making a more challenging test, Princeton adopted it for an admissions requirement (Owen). In 1925 Brigham developed the Scholastic Aptitude Test (SAT) for the College Board, adapting it directly from the Army Alpha and the modification he had used at Princeton (Owen). It was called an aptitude test to distinguish it from achievement tests currently used by the College Board (Crouse & Trusheim). Also, though his commission stated the SAT had reference to intelligence tests, they did not claim it measured intelligence (Crouse & Trusheim), and Brigham avoided calling it an "intelligence" test (Carroll). The first edition, containing antonyms, analogies, completions, and comprehension segments, was very similar to the modern SAT (Owen).

The SAT was first administered in 1926 (Crouse & Trusheim, 1988), and later adopted as a regular part of the College Board's admissions testing program in 1937 (Carroll, 1982). Use of the SAT grew little in the 1920s and 1930s, partly due to the effect of the Great Depression upon college enrollment (Crouse & Trusheim). The scale was readjusted each year, until April 1941, when it was standardized based on the performance of a standardization group of 10,654 students (Carroll). After this the College Board began equating each test by linking it statistically with the two that preceded it to provide the uniformity necessary for comparisons to be made between scores of students tested at different administrations (Owen, 1985). The SAT was renormed in April 1995; the scale was recentered by setting mean scores at 500, the midpoint of the 200-800 scale (College Board, 1999).

Each edition of the SAT was developed by Brigham and his staff at Princeton until his death in 1943 (Carroll, 1982). After the war, there was a great demand for admissions tests and use of the SAT increased dramatically (Owen, 1985). This was due to the increase in number of applicants, many of whom were veterans utilizing the G.I. Bill, and some colleges' desire to be selective (Crouse & Trusheim, 1988). In 1947 the College Board established the Educational Testing Service (ETS) to take over test preparation and scoring (Crouse & Trusheim). Its formation had been suggested by James B. Conant, then president of Harvard, and the staff of the late Brigham was merged in order to form the ETS (Carroll).

Henry Chauncey was the first ETS president (Owen, 1985) and James B. Conant became the first chairman of its board of trustees (Crouse & Trusheim, 1988). Chauncey saw the SAT as an IQ test (Owen), unlike its creator, Brigham. Besides using the SAT as an admission exam, Chauncey believed in other utilizations of intelligence tests in education. In 1951 Chauncey wrote in his annual report to the board of trustees that students should be tested in the eighth or ninth grade in order to guide them into certain vocational areas (as cited in Owen). Chauncey had said in his previous annual report that the hopes of low scorers should be kept "within reasonable bounds" (as cited in Crouse & Trusheim, p. 32). Conant advocated the use of intelligence tests to group high school students by ability, stating in 1959 that only 15 to 20% had the talent necessary for college (as cited in Carroll, 1982). This illustrated both men's acceptance of the still lingering presumption that IQ reflected a fixed intelligence that could not be changed (Carroll). In short, they were hereditarians who had not learned the lessons of Goddard, Terman, and Brigham before them.

Meritocracy

The views Chauncey and Conant supported involved one of the premises of hereditarianism: that a person's achievements and wealth be correlated with IQ (Gould, 1995). Earlier, Terman stated that IQ minimums could be set for occupations (e.g., 75 for unskilled laborers), but in a 1919 study (as cited in Gould, 1981), he found unskilled workers to have a mean IQ of 95, demonstrating that other factors besides intelligence play a role in career choice. Goddard had also seen test scores as a way of determining success, stating in 1919 that a person with a mental age of 20 should have a better home than someone with a mental age of 10 (as cited in Owen, 1985). This doctrine began to be carried out by Chauncey and Conant through the use of the SAT for admission to selective universities, and therefore into wealthier vocations. Chauncey saw ETS and its tests as regulators of access to institutions and professions; ensuring that the deserving succeeded while the undeserving did not (Owen). Their philosophy came to be known as meritocracy, a term invented by British sociologist Michael Young in the late 1950s, and defined by Owen as "a social hierarchy in which status and opportunity are determined by individual 'worth' rather than by, say, family lineage" (p. 197). Chauncey stated in 1961 that "justice should be done each individual according to his merit" (as cited in Owen, p. 198). That meritocracy became a widespread philosophy was evident due to the tenfold increase in number of SAT candidates from 1951 to 1961 (Crouse & Trusheim, 1988). Also, E. F. Lindquist founded the American College Testing Program (ACT) in 1959 after resigning from the CEEB (Carroll, 1982). The ACT measures achievement in English, mathematics, social studies, and natural sciences. It became the chief competitor of the SAT (Crouse & Trusheim), and it better reflects high school curricula (Owen).

The vast majority of colleges and universities were, and remain, basically unselective. So in those institutions the SAT did not determine admission. Only around 50 of 2000 or so institutions today are selective (Owen, 1985). In those that are selective, it is usually based on an aptitude test, most often the SAT (Crouse & Trusheim, 1988). This policy of meritocracy follows the early suggestion by Rogers (1922) that an institution use a test for student selection in order to maintain a high reputation. Few institutions use SAT scores alone to make admission decisions (Crouse & Trusheim). Most follow the advice of both the College Board and ETS not to base admission decisions solely on SAT scores (Carroll, 1982). Taking high school transcripts into consideration improves prediction of freshman grades (Crouse & Trusheim). The majority of colleges accept a high proportion of their applicants, and the College Board suggests students use their SAT scores to select a college in the first place (Crouse & Trusheim). However, rather than increasing enrollment with increased demand, the elite universities raise admission standards and become even more selective, with the end result that "the amount of room at the top of American universities is fixed" (Crouse & Trusheim, p. 37).

The idea that admission to elite institutions should be based on merit rather than wealth or other social considerations was certainly revolutionary in the 1950s. However, merit was defined by SAT scores and, in what could be characterized as their own recantation, ETS acknowledged that impoverished backgrounds and resulting different educational, cultural, and social opportunities caused some groups to have lower SAT averages than others (Crouse & Trusheim, 1988). With the Civil Rights Act of 1964, and the accompanying civil rights movement, some of these inequities in educational opportunities began to be erased (Snow & Yalow, 1982). ETS advocated the use of the SAT as a means to indicate where unequal opportunities existed (Crouse & Trusheim). Desegregation also played a role in giving racial groups equal educational opportunities. However, as long as there are inner-city versus suburban, rural versus urban, and public versus private schools that are funded differently, staffed with a different caliber of teachers, and have a different racial composition, then true equity in education will not be attained.

Meritocracy remained under fire in the 1980s. Owen (1985) stated that, in America's "classless" society, "tests like the SAT convert the tainted advantages of birth and wealth into the neutral currency of merit" (p. 266). Therefore, Owen wrote that " 'merit' is little more than camouflage for class" (p. 198). When ETS finally released data concerning race and SAT scores in 1981, it was found that African Americans and Whites scored differently and that this lowered the percentage of eligible African Americans at universities that used the SAT for selection (Crouse & Trusheim, 1988). To achieve a diverse enrollment, affirmative action was utilized to set aside strict score cutoffs, and the National Center for Fair and Open Testing was established in 1985 to guard against racial bias on the SAT (Crouse & Trusheim). Because of these issues concerning racial groups, Owen believed that meritocracy was not egalitarian and that it carried forward old injustices, even stating that "the meritocracy, as interpreted by ETS, is eugenics by other means" (p. 199). As a hypothesis for the racial disparity, Owen stated that the SAT was not a fair measure for African Americans, or other disadvantaged social groups, because the questions reflect the perspective, and, hence, culture, of upper-middle class Whites.

Strivers Score

Recently the ETS developed a "Strivers" score to take socioeconomic background and race of the test-taker into account on the SAT (Glazer & Thernstrom, 1999). As the title of Glazer and Thernstrom's article indicates, this could be "the end of meritocracy." The Strivers score is an adjustment of the actual SAT score, and is based on the fact that students from wealthier and better educated families, from high-income suburbs, and from better high schools score higher on average than students from poorer and less-educated families, which is the situation of a disproportionate number of minority students (Glazer & Thernstrom). This new score takes into consideration at least 14 factors that affect SAT scores and is designed to aid students who have scored higher than their demographic background would predict (Glazer & Thernstrom). The ACT program is also developing such a system (Glazer & Thernstrom).

This Strivers score is especially important because few institutions use family income as a factor in admissions decisions (Crouse & Trusheim, 1988), and because some policies of affirmative action have come under attack. Glazer and Thernstrom (1999) state that race remains a factor in test scores, particularly for African Americans, independent of economic and educational factors. Because there is no evidence to support any genetic hypothesis, this difference must then be due to the cultural factors discussed earlier with the SAT and intelligence tests. In spite of this, affirmative action programs have suffered through court decisions and popular referenda that have prevented any consideration based on racial background in admissions decisions in the states of Texas, California, and Washington (Glazer & Thernstrom). Currently, the Florida state legislature is considering Governor Jeb Bush's "One Florida" plan, which would also end consideration of race in admissions to its state universities (Crystal, 2000).

Like affirmative action, the Strivers project may face similar criticism and attacks. In fact, Glazer and Thernstrom's (1999) article is a debate about the Strivers program, with Glazer in favor and Thernstrom in opposition. Surveys show that university faculty members are strongly committed to keeping a diverse student body, as are administrators and state legislators (Glazer & Thernstrom). The introduction of the Strivers score by ETS should be instrumental in maintaining a racially diverse enrollment in all institutions of higher education. Also, with the Strivers adjustment, the SAT will be more in line with Binet's original vision of an academic test as a diagnostic instrument, rather than as an obstacle to collegiate admission.

Developmental Education

In the early part of the twentieth century, during the heyday of the hereditarian philosophy, there had been a few who advocated test use in accordance with Binet's example. Rogers (1922) suggested that colleges place freshmen in appropriate English courses based on their reading and language ability. Rogers also stated that with college entrants:

> It may be found that the individuals under consideration have remediable deficiencies, which require special attention, such as poor methods of learning. . . . Lack of capacity has often been assigned as a cause for what is really to be attributed to defective training and limited past experience. (pp. 249-250)

Freeman (1926) advocated the use of testing as a diagnostic tool when a student failed a course, stating tests have been used to determine the type of remedial work necessary so the student can be successful. In the Progressive Education Association's Eight Year Study (1932-1940) (cited in Crouse & Trusheim, 1988), a few hundred colleges waived their admissions policies for graduates of schools in the study, and results showed they did well in college. With the Civil Rights Act of 1964, there was an influx of students similar to that following World War II. Institutions with open admissions policies then had a substantial number of students who were underprepared (Wyatt, 1992) due to their lack of educational opportunity. In response, state governments began to mandate testing for placement and remediation (Crouse & Trusheim). Learning centers in community colleges started in the 1970s, and developmental programs became widespread in universities during the 1980s (Wyatt). Finally, tests were being used in colleges and universities the way Alfred Binet first intended, to ameliorate any academic deficiency.

Recently, some of the same state legislatures that mandated remedial and developmental programs have now scaled them back or cut them altogether at some colleges and universities. The City Universities of New York (CUNY) adopted a policy that limits remedial education exclusively to its two-year institutions (Cronholm, 1999). Cronholm was president of CUNY's Baruch College when it removed remedial courses in 1998 and supports such action in her article. (Because the term "developmental" is never used by Cronholm, her use of "remedial" will generally be followed in regard to her article, even though she may have incorrectly equated "remedial" with "developmental.") In her opinion, the successes of remedial students do not justify the investment by institutions in remediation. Cronholm stated that lower curriculum standards and grade inflation were among the costs to institutions. However, those claims cannot be substantiated. Including remedial and developmental courses, in addition to the regular curriculum, to help students in need, has no effect upon the "standards" in nondevelopmental courses. Furthermore, grade inflation has occurred in most colleges starting in the 1960s (Crouse & Trusheim, 1988), long before remedial and developmental courses were offered at many institutions.

Among other non sequiturs, Cronholm (1999) stated that remediation has a "demoralizing" effect upon "well-prepared" students who are in the same classes as remedial students. It is almost as if any remedial student is seen as wearing a scarlet "R." However, nondevelopmental students are not in remedial classes. Furthermore, because no distinction is made among students in other classes, nondevelopmental students would not even know if some of their classmates were remedial students, much less be demoralized. Such a statement about the demoralizing effect of the presence of remedial students also shows that, unfortunately, Binet's fears about their being pre-judged and labeled were well founded. Cronholm also wrote that remediation hurts developmental students because they often fail the college-level classes they must take in conjunction with remedial courses for full-time status. Exact statistics are not given for how often this occurs, but, stipulating the point, it seems to go against the earlier claim that grade inflation was due to the presence of remedial students and programs. Although failure is unpleasant, not having even the opportunity for success is certainly worse, and that is basically what is suggested at the article's conclusion.

After claiming that 20 years of reform efforts in kindergarten through 12th grade have not worked, Cronholm states that "the only way we can change the status quo — and the current excessive need for remediation of high-school graduates — is to reserve college for those who can do college-level work" (1999, p. B6). In other words, by denying admission to students not meeting requirements, Cronholm believes high schools will adjust their standards so their graduates can attend college. However, denying the students who attended poor high schools admission to college does not seem to be the answer. The individual graduates would be penalized, but the high school would not be held accountable. Cronholm's suggestion, if implemented, would use admissions tests in the manner of exclusion originated by Columbia University, without taking crucial background factors, like those cited in the Strivers index, into consideration.

Conclusion

The removal of remedial and developmental education programs from the four-year institutions of the City Universities of New York, and actions like this, effectively shut the door of opportunity to those who do not score well on admissions tests like the SAT. Advocates of such policies resemble the hereditarians of the past who shut the "golden door" of opportunity into this country to immigrants because of the elitist belief that recent immigrants' low test scores meant they would not be successful. Goddard, Terman, and Brigham recanted their hereditarian beliefs and came around to Binet's point of view. Hopefully supporters of admissions policies that exclude people will also change their views and accept Binet's position that tests should be used for inclusion, to determine if, and in what subject, someone admitted to college needs remediation. To those who persist in the belief that a low test score represents a permanent condition, and that the student can never succeed in college, developmental educators can respond as Binet did in a 1905 article:

> Never! What a momentous word. Some recent thinkers seem to have given their moral support to these deplorable verdicts by affirming that an individual's intelligence is a fixed quantity, a quantity that cannot be increased. We must protest and react against this brutal pessimism; we must try to demonstrate that it is founded upon nothing. (as cited in Gould, 1995, p. 18)

Binet's statements regarding the school children he helped through remediation beginning in 1904 are just as true for the college students enabled through developmental education programs today. Nearly 100 years after Binet invented aptitude tests, developmental educators still use them as he intended. A low SAT or ACT score does not mean an individual is not capable of learning college-level material; it just indicates the need for developmental instruction. Gould (1995) sees the distortion of Binet's humane efforts by hereditarians and eugenicists as "one of the great tragedies of twentieth-century science" (p. 17). To avoid a similar tragedy in twenty-first century education, there should always be a place for students needing remediation, and the developmental education programs that help them, in institutions of higher learning.

References

Carroll, J.B. (1982). The measurement of intelligence. In R.J. Sternberg (Ed.), *Handbook of human intelligence* (pp. 29-122). Cambridge, UK: Cambridge University.

College Board. (1999, August 31). *SAT table 1: Average SAT scores of entering college classes, 1967-1999* [Online]. Available: http://www.collegeboard.org/index_this/press/senior99/html/satt1.html

Cronholm, L. (1999, September 24). Why one college jettisoned all its remedial courses. *The Chronicle of Higher Education*, p. B6.

Crouse, J., & Trusheim, D. (1988). *The case against the SAT*. Chicago: The University of Chicago.

Crystal, L.M. (Executive Producer). (2000, March 7). *The news hour with Jim Lehrer*. New York: Public Broadcasting Service.

Freeman, F.N. (1926). *Mental tests: Their history, principles, and applications*. Boston: Houghton Mifflin.

Glazer, N., & Thernstrom, A. (1999, September 27). The end of meritocracy: Should the SAT account for race? *The New Republic, 221*, 26-29.

Goodenough, F.L. (1949). *Mental testing: Its history, principles, and applications*. New York: Rinehart.

Gould, S.J. (1981). *The mismeasure of man*. New York: W. W. Norton.

Gould, S.J. (1995, February). Ghosts of bell curves past. *Natural History, 104*, 12-19.

Gould, S.J. (1998, March). The internal brand of the scarlet W. *Natural History, 107*, 22-25, 70-78.

Herrnstein, R.J., & Murray, C.A. (1994). *The bell curve: Intelligence and class structure in American life*. New York: Free Press.

Laboratory of Comparative Human Cognition. (1982). Culture and intelligence. In R.J. Sternberg (Ed.), *Handbook of human intelligence* (pp. 642-719). Cambridge, UK: Cambridge University.

Miller, W.S. (1922). The administrative use of intelligence tests in the high school. In G.M. Whipple (Ed.), *The twenty-first yearbook of the National Society for the Study of Education: Intelligence tests and their use* (pp. 189-222). Bloomington, IL: Public School Publishing.

Owen, D. (1985). *None of the above: Behind the myth of scholastic aptitude*. Boston: Houghton Mifflin.

Pintner, R. (1922). The significance of intelligence testing in the elementary school. In G.M. Whipple (Ed.), *The twenty-first yearbook of the National Society for the Study of Education: Intelligence tests and their use* (pp. 153-167). Bloomington, IL: Public School Publishing.

Rogers, A.L. (1922). The use of psychological tests in the administration of colleges of liberal arts for women. In G.M. Whipple (Ed.), *The twenty-first yearbook of the National Society for the Study of Education: Intelligence tests and their use* (pp. 245-252). Bloomington, IL: Public School Publishing.

Scarr, S., & Carter-Saltzmann, L. (1982). Genetics and intelligence. In R.J. Sternberg (Ed.), *Handbook of human intelligence* (pp. 792-896). Cambridge, UK: Cambridge University.

Snow, R.E., & Yalow, E. (1982). Education and intelligence. In R.J. Sternberg (Ed.), *Handbook of human intelligence* (pp. 493-585). Cambridge, UK: Cambridge University.

Trachtenberg, M. (1976). *The statue of liberty*. New York: Viking.

Whipple, G.M. (1922). Intelligence tests in colleges and universities. In G.M. Whipple (Ed.), *The twenty-first yearbook of the National Society for the Study of Education: Intelligence tests and their use* (pp. 253-270). Bloomington, IL: Public School Publishing.

Wyatt, M. (1992). The past, present, and future need for college reading courses. *U.S. Journal of Reading, 36*(1), 10-20.

The Relationship Between Concept
of Intelligence and Teacher Goals

Linda Maitland
Klien Independent School District

Abstract

This qualitative case study explores how a teacher's thinking becomes apparent in her teaching practice. Specifically, this study found that a teacher's conception of intelligence is reflected in her goals for students. Current research indicates that teachers' classroom behavior is, at least in part, determined by their concept of intelligence. A continuum of views concerning the conceptualization of intelligence is presented. Research is reviewed that illustrates how teacher conceptualization of intelligence impacts teaching and learning. The findings of this study coincide with previous research that demonstrates a relationship between teacher beliefs and teaching practice. This research concludes that knowledge of teacher conceptualization of intelligence could impact school reform and the learning success of underachievers.

The daily task of the teacher is vitally complex and challenging. A teacher must constantly sense and interpret any combination of variables: student needs, curricular decisions, social issues, timing, discipline, emotional factors, and the institution's and the community's learning requirements. The art of teaching involves continual negotiation between the institutional context and a complexity of student needs. These play out against the

For additional information contact: Linda Maitland • Klien Independent School District • 7826 Green Lawn Drive • Houston, TX 77088 • e-mail: lmaitland@pdq.net background of the personal experience and beliefs of the teacher. This study aims to simplify the complex work of teaching by isolating one factor, the concept of intelligence, and exploring its relationship to teacher behaviors. The researcher chose to study the conceptualization of intelligence because intelligence is endemic to education and is of prime interest to those concerned with learning. One's understanding of intelligence, therefore, is fundamental to the work of teaching and to what occurs in classrooms at all levels.

The targeted setting was a college developmental reading classroom because it offered an opportunity to consider elements that contribute to understanding how underprepared students make academic gains. According to Boylan and Bonham (1992), developmental learners are as likely to persist and graduate as their more advanced counterparts, and 83 % of students who pass their developmental reading course also pass their first reading-based social science course.

Therefore, the college developmental reading classroom was studied because it might tangentially contribute to understanding how the underprepared become successful learners.

The research question for this study is how might a college developmental reading teacher's belief concerning intelligence affect her goals for students? First, the conceptualization of intelligence is reviewed, including an overview of research that explores how a teacher's concept of intelligence can impact classroom practice. Second, the study ascertains the teacher's conceptualization of intelligence. Next, the teacher's concept of intelligence is revealed, and her actions in the classroom are presented. Finally, the study becomes an opportunity to consider the consequences of teacher beliefs.

Theoretical Foundations

Teacher Thinking

The first premise of this exploration involves a branch of research that studies the mental processes of teachers and the resulting classroom practices. Good and Brophy (1991) wrote that a teacher's behavior is naturally shaped by his or her thinking: "Teachers' behavior is goal-directed and thus shaped by their beliefs" (p.10). Similarly, Clark and Peterson (1986) noted that teacher behavior is directed by a personal system of beliefs, values, and principles. Wadsworth (1989) theorized that a teacher's concept of intelligence is one of the most important determiners of teacher behaviors. Similarly, Nicholls, Patashnick, and Metteal (1986) stated that teachers' decision-making regarding classroom methods is influenced by how they perceive intelligence.

How Intelligence is Conceptualized

Defining intelligence is problematic and debatable. Historically the argument has centered around two questions: (a) is heredity or environment the determiner of intelligence? and (b) is intelligence defined or determined as a unitary factor, or is it a combination of factors? Collier (1994) summarized that there is no one accepted definition of intelligence, no agreement on how it should be measured, and no consensus concerning which could have greater impact on intelligence, heredity or environment.

Terminology concerning intelligence is confusing, and their questions are endless. For example, many people use the term intelligence quotient (IQ) and the word intelligence as synonyms. One theorist (Meyer, 1982) referred to "splitters" and "lumpers," or those who believe intelligence is multifaceted, contrasted with those who believe it is based on one underlying factor. Conceptualization of intelligence has perplexed both children and adults (Dweck & Bempechat, 1983; Sternberg, 1985). Is it age related? Is intelligence in one culture something else in another culture? Are some generations more intelligent than other generations? The intelligence construct is a conceptual and semantic challenge. For the purposes of this study, the terminology of Dweck and Elliott (1983) is utilized. Dweck and Elliott conceptualize intelligence as a continuum, with the entity perspective at one end of the continuum and the incremental perspective at the other end.

The entity view of intelligence perceives intelligence as a singular characteristic. The idea stems from the 1900s when Binet and Simon (1905) devised a method to identify "retarded" children for special placement. Along this vein, Spearman (1927) proposed that the "g" factor was a unitary construct underscoring all abilities. The entity perspective explains that intelligence is an inborn ability that can be measured by math and language skills such as those tested in IQ tests. Words such as holistic, innate, and unchangeable describe this view.

Other theorists described the incremental view of intelligence as multifaceted, malleable, and effort related. Cattell (1963, 1971) proposed that intelligence was double-faceted: (a) crystallized intelligence was culturally influenced, fact oriented, and dependent upon math, vocabulary, and general information, whereas (b) fluid intelligence was perceived as an ability to see relationships and solve problems. Gardner (1983) extended thinking about intelligence as multifaceted by explaining that there are seven different kinds of intelligence (linguistic, logical-mathematical, musical, bodily-kinesthetic, spatial, interpersonal, and intrapersonal), with individuals having strengths in some components and weaknesses in others. Another theorist, Sternberg (1985, 1988), discussed intelligence from what he called a "triarchic" approach. First, he said intelligence must be understood within its sociocultural context. Next, intelligence is demonstrated by our adaptations to something learned. Third, he theorized that intelligence involved the application of behaviors, such as information processing, the implementation of appropriate strategies, and knowledge acquisition. Last, Collier (1994) reported that motivation influences cognition, and that intrinsic motivation, achievement motivation, high aspirations, and an internal locus of control all impinge upon the use and development of cognitive skills.

How Conceptualization of Intelligence Is Related to Goals

To summarize, the intelligence continuum has, at one pole, the entity conceptualization of intelligence, which perceives intelligence as an inborn, fixed, global ability. At the other pole is the incremental conceptualization, which perceives intelligence as a range of abilities that are malleable and environmentally influenced. How might such different points of view be related to teacher classroom practice? Current research has explored the impact of the concept of intelligence on teaching and learning. Studies have concluded that one's understanding of intelligence might influence learning goals, motivation, the evaluation of what is learned, the perception of what brings about learning, the selection of teaching methods, and one's beliefs about the nature of knowledge. For example, researchers have found that the conceptualization of intelligence impacts the kinds of goals learners set. Those who ascribe to the entity conceptualization of intelligence adopt performance goals, while those who ascribe to the incremental concept adopt mastery goals (Ames, 1992; Dweck, 1986; Dweck and Elliott, 1983; Dweck & Leggett, 1988).

Performance goals are ability related, whereas mastery goals are effort related. With performance goals, learning is a means to an end, and the product is the focus. With mastery goals, learning in and of itself is valued; in other words, the process is important. Performance goals are associated with competition and comparison with others (i.e., norm referenced) while mastery goals are self-referenced (Slate, Jones, & Charlesworth, 1990). According to Garner (1990), because mastery goal learning is related to effort, failure can be remedied with persistence and the application of more effective strategies. Mastery goal proponents perceive intelligence as something that can develop over time and improve as the learner takes on challenges. Because performance goals are ability related, a learner's self-concept may become threatened and, as a result, further learning may be discouraged. Some learners, referred to as the "learned-helpless," may give up in the face of challenge while others continue to be motivated despite failure. According to current theory, these performance-threatened learners may avoid challenge and use short-term learning strategies such as memorization. But learners with mastery goals, who attribute outcomes to learning strategy employed or effort expended, may increase achievement behavior, demonstrating how motivation rather than intelligence impacts behavior (Ames, 1992; Dweck, 1986; Dweck & Elliott, 1983; Dweck & Leggett, 1988; Pintrich & DeGroot, 1990; Ryan & Grolnick, 1986).

Perry (1968) theorized that one's conceptualization of knowledge is related to one's conceptualization of intelligence. He proposed that there exists a spectrum of beliefs about knowledge: (a) from knowledge as a dualistic, absolute right or wrong determined by an authority, agreeable with an entity conceptualization of intelligence, to (b) knowledge as relative to a context, agreeable with an incremental conceptualization of intelligence. A number of studies (Slate et al., 1990; Wadsworth, 1989; Nicholls, et al., 1986) explain that one's beliefs about the nature of knowledge are associated with particular classroom methods. Slate, Jones, and Charlesworth theorized that teachers who ascribe to a dualistic belief of knowledge, as do entity teachers, will value "rote learning of a fixed truth" (p.26). These teachers will present material in a single method, and they will maintain control of goals and standards. Additionally, entity teachers will use norm-referenced grading, perceive error as failure, reward success more than they reward progress, and they will have high expectations for high-ability learners. Study habits are of less importance to entity teachers because learning is attributed to an innate ability (Slate, et al.). Additionally, according to Covington and Omelich (1979), effort and hard work are negatively related because success at learning comes so easily to the bright. Teachers who ascribe to thinking that knowledge is relative and contextual, as do incremental teachers, will lean toward different kinds of classroom practices. They employ a variety of teaching methods, reward progress, emphasize good study habits, provide opportunities for practice and rehearsal of new learning, stress critical thinking, accept error as a natural part of learning, use criterion-referenced grading, have high expectations for all students, encourage students to set their own goals and standards, and emphasize cooperation (Slate, et al.). Thus, the concept of intelligence appears related to teaching and learning in numerous important ways.

Figure 1. Summary of the continuum of intelligence and Its associated classroom practices.

How is intelligence conceptualized?	Entity = heredity based • Fixed, unchanging • Global, unitary factor •An innate gift • IQ determined	Incremental = environment influenced • Malleable • A range of abilities • Grows with effort
What is the nature of knowledge?	Dualistic • Determined by an outside authority • Teacher controls standards • Error = related to failure • Norm-referenced	Pluralistic • Relative to context • A reasoned truth, error = a natural part of learning • Self-referenced • Learner control
How are goals described?	Performance goals = ability related • Rewards the end product • Competition • Failure = reflects upon ability and self-concept	Mastery goals = effort • Values the process and steps • Rewards the effort • Cooperation • Failure = remedy with new strategies and persistence
What are other teaching and learning associations?	Lesson presented in a single method • Rote learning of basics, facts • Math and language oriented	Lessons presented in a variety of methods • Information processing • Critical thinking • Solve problems • See relationships

Figure 1 summarizes the theoretical foundations of this study. A continuum of the conceptualization of intelligence is represented as it is related to a continuum of teaching and learning behaviors. Certainly teachers vary greatly as to where (and to the degree or extent) they fall within the continuum, with no one teacher falling totally toward one side of the spectrum and not the other.

Method

A qualitative case study was selected as the appropriate design suited to the researcher's purpose, which was to investigate "motives and aims, not just the behavior" (Sherman & Webb, 1988) of those studied. Multiple data sources, such as interviews, audio tapes, observation, documents, an assessment instrument, and outside raters, provided triangulation and reliability. Documents collected were the syllabus, grade book, attendance records, hand-outs, teacher plans, texts, student work, folders, and e-mails. Goetz and LeCompte (1984) noted that documents may inform what is not observable, and Eisner (1991) explained that documents can "provide a kind of definition of what teachers value" (p. 184).

Data Collection and Analysis

Data management and analysis were nonlinear and recursive. The processes involved combing through the data looking for patterns, domains, and categories that emerged (Spradley, 1980). Goetz and LeCompte (1984) noted that data collection and analysis are linked in qualitative research, and that the researcher may formulate questions after "initial impressions and perceptions have been analyzed and tentative conclusions have been formulated" (p. 165). Interviews were audio taped while notes were taken simultaneously. Successive interviews evolved from the general to the more detailed and specific (Spradley, 1979).

Setting

This study was conducted at an open-admissions, two-year branch campus. The college, which is about 40 years old, was located in a rural-industrial, midwestern community with a population of 54,000. The institution was regarded as integral to the economic recovery of a community that suffered from setbacks in the steel industry.

This campus' developmental program has been in place for over 20 years. As part of the admissions process, entering freshmen were tested in basic skills, and those students whose scores indicated need were enrolled in developmental classes in reading, writing, or math. Developmental classes were mandatory for most students, and grades calculated as part of the grade point average, but these courses could not be applied toward degree credit. Regular credit-bearing classes could be taken concurrently with developmental course work. Developmental class size was limited to 25 students.

The College Reading and Study Skills summer course provided this study's data. Classes met two days a week for two and one half hours over eight weeks. The College Reading and Study Skills course, designed to help students improve and practice college-level reading comprehension, covered a broad range of study skills, such as note taking, test taking, text marking and underlining, and other strategies for effective learning in college. There was no exit test. The course goal was to prepare students to succeed in college level work. Before each class, as requested by the teacher, the students arranged their desks in a circle. Student folders, which contained daily assignments and corrected work, were placed on a long table near the door so students could check their progress and read teacher comments upon arrival.

The Participants

The students in the class reflected a range of diversity in age, economic circumstances, work experience, and educational background. There were nonnative English speakers, a hearing-impaired student who was accompanied each day by an interpreter, and a high school student. The racial mix of White, Asian, and African-Americans presented a broad cultural picture.

The teacher in this study had seven years of experience in the field of developmental education. The researcher selected this teacher because within the seven branches of this university, she was highly respected by her peers. She taught two developmental reading classes per semester, while pursuing a doctoral degree in developmental education at a nearby major research university. She could be described as a highly reflective teaching professional: she kept personal journals of her teaching; she stayed well-informed with teaching practices and trends through her doctoral coursework and reading in publications and journals; she attended conferences of local and national teaching and research organizations; and she maintained memberships in professional organizations related to reading and developmental education.

Procedures for Assessment of Intelligence

A vignette (Figure 2) and a focused free write (Figure 3) were devised to ascertain the teacher's concept of intelligence. After the completion of the summer session, the teacher was asked to respond in writing to the vignette and to the free write. Three independent raters, all teaching professionals who did not know the individual, evaluated the teacher's responses.

Figure 2. The Vignette

Read the following vignette. Afterwards, please respond in writing with your thoughts.

The semester is underway. You've had a chance to interact with your class, and you've seen the work students can do. You feel confident that you have some grasp on the learners' strengths and weaknesses, and your lessons are appropriate to meet their needs.You must describe a bright student in this class and tell how you recognize his or her intelligence. How would you recognize and describe your less bright student? How would you gear your teaching for these diverse students?

Figure 3. The Focused Free write

Please respond informally in writing:

> Some teachers believe that a student's IQ has a definite influence on achievement. Others
> believe that intelligence can change over time and is affected by effort, learning, and other
> variables. One modern theorist talks about people having "multiple intelligences"; in
> other words, people have talents in some areas but not in other areas. What is your view
> of intelligence?

Findings

Results of Assessment of Intelligence

The three teacher raters concluded that the teacher's concept of intelligence fit with the incremental view of intelligence. Each rater supported her conclusion by citing from the teacher's written responses. For example, one rater assessed the teacher's comment concerning "providing a variety of avenues to learn" as fitting with the incremental view of intelligence. Another rater found that the teacher linked intelligence to learning that depended on student commitment and persistence when she wrote, "students who are willing to work do learn and grow." The third rater listed the following responses as favoring the incremental view of intelligence: "comes prepared . . . attends regularly . . . participates in class activities . . . contributes in discussions . . . turns assignments in on time . . . takes pride in work . . . is committed to school as is evident by a determination to do his/her best." The conclusion of the three raters was that this teacher's conceptualization of intelligence coincided with the incremental model. The next step was to examine the teacher's goals for students and her actions in the classroom.

Teacher Goal #1: Pedagogy

The teacher's pedagogical goals for students stemmed from two schools of thought. It is through these two pedagogical approaches that we gain knowledge about what the teacher valued. These are the foundations that drove her teaching methods and curriculum delivery. The first was reader response theory, and the second was whole language.

Reader response theory posits that reading is an interaction between the reader and the text, and that meaning is constructed as the reader's own personal experience interacts with the words of the text (Winterowd, 1989). In other words, the teacher wants her students to connect their schema, their knowledge and experience, to the curriculum. When this is achieved, students' reading becomes applicable and relevant on a personal level. For example, the researcher observed that from one reading the students were asked to explain how they might have responded differently to the problem of the character in the reading. In another instance, to encourage a personal connection to learning, the teacher asked open-ended questions to stimulate reflection, and she challenged students to refine and expand their thinking by asking probing questions. As differing points of view surfaced during class discussions, students were required to support their statements with factual details and reasoning from their own lives and awareness. The teacher explained that this kind of an open forum of idea sharing was, for her, the essence of learning in higher education.

The teacher's second pedagogical approach is based in whole language theory. Although this method is often associated with primary education, the teacher felt there existed a connection to college reading. Whole language integrates learning within meaningful contexts (Vacca & Vacca, 1993), whereas in phonics the approach would be skill based. The teacher's curriculum did not include practicing isolated reading skills such as, tone or author's point of view, but occasionally did include what she called "mini-lessons," which were lessons she categorized as coming from the phonics perspective because of their focus on specific isolated topics. When she found a student, or several students, consistently making errors in an isolated area, she provided instruction. "I let some things ride, but I don't let everything ride. I try to instruct as much as they will be able to handle at one time." She did this individually with students during office hours, privately in their class folders, or in small groups.

Assignments were not limited only to reading, but involved listening, speaking, and writing. Fjeldstad (1994) described whole language:

> [Whole language focuses] on content rather than on a skill and process. Reading fluently is not the laborious assembling of a set of discrete skills (for example, finding the main idea, drawing an inference, etc.) independent of context. If you had to learn to play a game of tennis by analyzing each stroke in detail, never putting the sections together and taking a satisfying whack at the ball, all interest in tennis would be quickly lost. This is the frustration many of our students have with reading. (p. xxiii)

Fjeldstad explained that the whole language approach to reading has students experience reading as an essential and pleasurable part of everyday living; learning to read better is attained by reading. Reading and writing are inextricably linked as students think and write about ideas from their reading. In this way students co-create their own version of the text and monitor their own understanding. Individuals must read to develop a knowledge base that facilitates further learning. This forms a background that lifts students from a beginning reader status.

Teacher Goal #2: Awareness and Respect for Learners

The teacher expressed that awareness and respect for students were fundamental to her teaching. Without these, learning would be limited. Curriculum and its delivery required knowledge of the learner. In order to meet student learning needs, her goal was to become aware of learner uniqueness. For example, awareness of student levels of proficiency, both student strengths and weaknesses, provided a guide to her teaching. With this awareness she could compensate for student learning differences and thereby reach all students. When teaching a student with a hearing impairment she commented,

I respect the fact that she needs more time to process information, so I try to be aware if I'm just carrying her along. When her interpreter asked that I pause between overheads, I respect that need and am pleased to accommodate.

At another time her awareness of student uniqueness was expressed:

With my English as a Second Language students, I realize that they are very able students but language can slow down their process. When I see quizzical looks on their faces, I try to restate a point using various synonyms or asking for student examples. This way I can increase their comprehension and have an opportunity to reinforce.

She explained that awareness and respect for students was necessary because she did not want to "turn any learner off [and] have them shutdown." This would impinge on their experience and learning in the classroom. "I think a good developmental teacher should first realize who her students are," and she added that a developmental teacher must be aware that when a statement is made in class, it can be interpreted in a variety of ways and that potentially "everyone is going to take it in a different way." She believed it was important to note student differences in order to realize commonalities shared by classmates. Her goal was to shed light on "the sameness we all share with each other, because sharing and collaboration are a big part of my class. I think we learn so much by being together."

Her respect for students was demonstrated by her actions. She focused her attention on the students when they were speaking, and she listened attentively. She tried to learn the students' names before the start of the second class. She was on time with due dates and promptly returned student work, and she respected student time by beginning and ending class punctually. Finally, she gave students personal one-on-one attention when needed, both in and out of class.

Teacher Goal #3: Promote Student Language

By promoting student language use the teacher encouraged a high degree of interaction: student to student, teacher to student, and student to teacher. As noted above, the teacher designed lessons that required the use of language by integrating reading, speaking, writing, and listening. Language use was required when students had to construct and express answers in their own words, rather than circle a multiple-choice answer. Communication took place in the following modes: e-mails, whole-class discussion, small-group discussion, one-on-one, in-class, in pairs, in journals, through notations on papers and projects, and in student class folders. Students were encouraged to put their thinking into words:

I give my students every opportunity to talk. I want them to express their ideas with other classmates. I want them to talk to me in class and out of class. They must be active participants and actively practice expressing themselves using language to communicate their thinking.

The teacher explained that one of the benefits of a focus on dialogue was to give students the opportunity to voice their opinions and have their statements refined by others. Another important aspect of classroom talk is that students learn more: "It lets them know that just because they think something, doesn't mean everyone thinks it. So they have an opportunity to see new perspectives."

Teacher Goal #4: Promote Student Confidence

The teacher expressed a desire to promote student confidence. This was accomplished by choosing lessons that were appropriately geared to a level that provided learning and required effort. She commented,

> If they come to me at this point in their lives, they have probably experienced some painful reading and learning experiences. The exception might be the older student returning to college to brush up on skills, so my work involves creating experiences that are pleasant and uplifting.

How did she build confidence in students with difficult histories? She explained, "I should provide success, realistic success, not overly-inflated." She did this by challenging them with lessons that were within their reach but required new ideas and strategies: "Every student can learn and grow because I'm working with them at their own level. There's nothing that is impossible for them to do, and if they have trouble, there's always another alternative for them." Persistence and effort were highly valued by the teacher.

The syllabus said that students had an opportunity to earn 230 points by accomplishing a variety of course projects: a literacy paper, vocabulary, journals, reading exercises, e-mail assignments, notebooks, newspaper reports, and other activities. Points were deducted for late work. In the past she had experimented with the practice of offering bonus points to encourage and motivate "the strugglers," but when she found that the students who did not need the points were earning them, while those who could have benefited from them did not, she discontinued the practice.

Teacher Goal #5: Promote Student Self-Awareness

The teacher's goal of promoting student self-awareness had two purposes. Students would become more aware of their strengths as learners, and additionally, their self-confidence as students would increase with the daily, personal, encouraging feedback from the teacher. The teacher expressed a desire for her students to become aware of the "talents and gifts" they possessed. The teacher was committed to providing students with opportunities to:

> discover their capabilities as learners. They may not realize their own proficiency in some area. For example, in writing, none of them think they can write when they come to class. I think that by encouraging them in their writing they feel more confident and are more apt to use this skill. Asking them to do things they never thought about doing before encourages them to think in new ways and see new perspectives.

Students were encouraged to become aware of themselves as learners. She asked that they monitor themselves and self-evaluate in reading, learning, and studying. Rather than ask for one literal correct answer, the teacher's questions required deeper processing. Self-awareness was required when she requested that students think and find meaningful relationships between their own schema and the lesson.

She asked that students share their mental processing of their thinking steps with classmates because she believed that self-monitoring and metacognition were crucial in reading. She modeled for students her internal mental dialogue of her own comprehension process. Students could observe her active, interactive process of reading as she made explicit the internal process that reading involved. Additionally, she asked that students model their internal thinking and comprehension. When comprehension broke down, she required students to model the break down, orally express what went awry, and make explicit the remedies they applied to get meaning. "Inner talk" became public as the teacher and her students made their mental processes explicit.

Another way the teacher encouraged self-awareness was to ask for student self-evaluation regarding lessons that were most beneficial for them. Her purpose was to get students to look at their own products and their own academic growth. She wanted students to become self-aware and recognize the quality and care they were investing or not investing in their work. As they self-assessed, they might feel guilty, wasteful, proud, confident, or any range of emotions, and she believed this was valuable learning academically and personally. Her goal guided students to "grade themselves," as an important step toward recognizing priorities, increasing self-awareness, and developing metacognition.

The teacher believed that every piece of work accomplished by each student had importance and value. Thus, assignments turned in were returned with a notation, grade, or comment. She recognized time or effort invested in each project, a challenge overcome, an interesting or unusual insight offered, progress made, or whatever else might encourage and motivate students to persevere in furthering their learning:

> I want them to know that what they do in class and out is important to me and so I write lots of comments. Projects and assignments warrant feedback. I don't want students to receive only a letter grade. They work hard, sometimes for hours, so I want to respond to them and make sure they understand the reason behind the grade they receive.

Another form of student self-awareness involved allowing the students an opportunity to experience what college requires of them. She explained that some students come to class faithfully and show responsibility in the way that they manage their work, but others "weed themselves out of college. They think they want to come, but then discover they really do not want to do what is asked of them." She felt that students must self-assess and become aware of their priorities: "Poor attendance, personal problems, illness, work schedules, children, all sorts of issues can come into the picture, and the student must become aware of priorities and organize around them. [sic]" About a student who was a single parent with a job that required him to attend a professional conference during class time, she commented:

> I figure it is probably going to be up to him to determine what his priorities are . . . I can see education is important for him, but perhaps now, this is the best he can do with the other

constraints on his time. I would hope he would better manage his time for school, but this is up to him, not me. I just want him to be aware of what's going on here, and I see he's trying.

Her comments reflected a respectful understanding of the lives of students, yet academic reality was not compromised.

Analyses of Findings

The problem was to examine how teacher conceptualization of intelligence became apparent in teacher action. Specifically, the purpose of this exploration was to ascertain how a teacher's view of intelligence was reflected in her goals for students. The analyses of data demonstrated that this teacher's incremental conceptualization of intelligence was abundantly apparent in her goals and classroom actions.

The incremental view of intelligence was clearly evident in the teacher's reader response and whole language pedagogical approaches to teaching. In reader response theory the emphasis is on the interaction between the student and the text: students construct their understanding of text by making connections to their own lives and schema. The researcher observed students shifting back and forth between personal, internal schema and the text, hypothesizing and comparing their life experiences with their reading. For example, students assumed the roles of story characters and expressed how they would respond to the story's dilemma in a different manner. Cattell (1963, 1971), from the incremental school, would acknowledge this as fluid intelligence, which is the ability to see relationships and solve problems. Cattell proposed that intelligence involved an ability to perceive relationships between things: reader response asks that readers perceive a relationship between their own lives and the text. Thus, teacher belief in the incremental view of intelligence coincided with her classroom practice.

Reader response does not ask for a solitary answer; rather, it allows the student the freedom to discuss a reading without fear that the one, right interpretation, known only to the teacher, will come crashing down on his or her head. In reader response there is no one correct answer "out there." The teacher relinquishes the role of sole authority, the know-it-all critic with the only right answers (Foster, 1994; Perry, 1968). Slate, Jones, and Charlesworth (1990) and Perry (1968) noted that incremental teachers design lessons where multiple answers are acceptable. Perry theorized that incremental teachers view right and wrong as something relative within a context, rather than as an absolute determined by an outside authority. This teacher's lessons encouraged students to think critically and share their thinking with classmates, while a progression of ideas, not one correct answer, was validated. Slate, Jones, and Charlesworth wrote that a "belief in a reasoned truth appears consistent with the emphasis on critical thinking in the incremental view" (p.26).

Another correspondence between reader response and incremental intelligence entails student awareness of internal mental processes. Sternberg (1985, 1988), from the incremental school, emphasized that intelligence involves a consciousness of the steps and strategies of thinking, as well as information processing and the application of appropriate strategies. Dweck

(1986), when discussing goals set by incremental teachers, showed that mastery learning involved goals that foster self-regulatory learning strategies. This teacher's emphasis on the metacognitive aspects of the reading process was observed as the teacher and students modeled their comprehension processes out loud, making explicit the steps readers go through as they construct meaning. The teacher encouraged students to be aware of their internal mental dialogue when she asked them to say aloud how they processed text, and when she asked them to remedy comprehension break-down by verbalizing their thinking out loud. She also modeled her own internal mental steps of her thinking processes. This teaching encouraged students to become metacognitive learners and to self-regulate in reading and thinking, and thus to monitor their problem solving strategies. Incremental intelligence attributes achievement in learning to strategies employed and emphasizes the internal processes of thinking (Sternberg, 1985, 1988; Weinberg, 1989). Again, teacher concept of intelligence was apparent in her classroom practice.

Another teacher goal was that students should develop self-awareness. The teacher stated that she wanted students to become aware of their areas of learning proficiencies. Incremental intelligence was apparent in the recognition of humans as multifaceted human beings with strengths in various domains (Gardner, 1983). The incremental perspective is highlighted by its alternative, for the entity view designates that a one global ability determines what is intelligent. This teacher, with her incremental perspective of intelligence, did not grade her students by comparing student outcomes to nationally normed test scores. There was no competition. Instead, student learning was self-referenced and evaluated by measuring the individual student's progress and growth. These teaching methods are strongly focused on the individual as learner and are, thus, related to the incremental conceptualization of intelligence (Dweck & Elliott, 1883; Nicholls, Patashnick, & Mattetal, 1986; Wadsworth, 1989).

Another goal, closely related to the two previous goals, had to do with the teacher's awareness and respect for her students. This became evident when she spoke of knowing her students' cultures, their levels of proficiency, and other idiosyncrasies that might influence their experience and learning in the classroom. Her respect for students was evident in numerous ways: in comments on student work, in her regard for their time, in her attentiveness to them, and in her value for student self-assessment of learning. She sought awareness of student uniqueness and difference in order to reach students appropriately. The incremental view of intelligence perceives learners as having strengths in some areas and weaknesses in others, a recognition of student uniqueness and difference. Gardner's (1983) concept of multiple intelligences recognized each learner's different levels and different proficiencies.

The teacher of this study ascribed to whole language theory of instruction, and consequently one of her instructional goals was to encourage writing, listening, and speaking, in addition to reading. She placed great importance on students as language users and sought to provide opportunities for them to practice expressing themselves. All students were engaged as users of language. Students had the opportunity to hear other points of view and to refine their thinking through discussion with others. Refining answers requires re-thinking and re-articulating. Imbedded here, also, is the idea that thinking can improve or erroneous thinking change, and those who ascribe to incremental intelligence accept error as a natural part of the learning process (Slate et al., 1990). In this same vein, some people give up when faced with a challenge (e.g., a wrong answer? an idea that needs fine-tuning?) because their self-esteem is threatened. Researchers have noted that people with performance goals may give up in the face of challenge, while those with mastery goals are more likely to persist. This teacher's focus on mastery goals are associated with the incremental conceptualization of intelligence (Dweck & Elliott, 1983; Dweck & Leggett, 1988; Paris & Newman, 1990; Pintrich & DeGroot, 1990). Again, teacher thinking coincided with teacher action.

The fourth goal was to develop student self-confidence. Previously discussed was the teacher's goal of knowing her students' proficiencies, weaknesses, and uniqueness as learners. With this knowledge the teacher designed lessons that were appropriately challenging and required student effort. As noted, incremental intelligence is aligned with student effort and persistence. Mastery learning research found that a pattern of achievement became reinforced as effort expended brought success (Paris & Newman, 1990; Pintrich & DeGroot, 1990). The teacher demonstrated repeatedly that she valued effort and persistence. For any student who was unable to complete an assignment but demonstrated effort and persistence, the teacher managed to find an alternate route to learning. This teacher goal, then, is agreeable to the incremental view of intelligence and its associated mastery learning practices.

Conclusion and Implications

The findings of this case study coincide with current and previous research that demonstrates that teacher behavior is shaped by teacher thinking (Good & Brophy, 1991). This study found that a teacher's conceptualization of intelligence is reflected in her goals for students. As a single factor, a teacher's conception of intelligence can impact and determine the scope and dimension of classroom organization and delivery of curriculum. Results of this study emphasize an important link between conceptualization of intelligence and teaching and learning processes. In other words, the mindset of the person doing the teaching is of prime significance.

Although this case study's focus was limited to one teacher, this study has implications for bringing about change in education. People are scrutinizing public education and they are critical of the job high schools and elementary schools are doing. The public wants a higher quality of education. They want changes in the schools. Because teacher conceptualization of intelligence is endemically related to what occurs in classrooms, one place to begin initiating change is to consider the thinking of teachers. Educational administrators, practicing teaching professionals, teachers in training, and institutions involved with the education of pre-service teachers all need to consider the important relationship between the conceptualization of intelligence and teachers' classroom behaviors. Without changes in teacher thinking, it may be impractical to consider making changes in the schools.

Another implication of this research has to do with personnel decisions in teaching. Because it appears that teacher conceptualization of intelligence impacts what happens in the classroom in numerous important ways, perhaps knowing a teacher's views concerning intelligence can provide clues as to which teachers would be most effective in particular classrooms. For example, in a high school that groups students heterogeneously for instruction, might a teacher who believes in incremental intelligence be a better teacher than one who favors the entity view of intelligence? How does teacher thinking fit with the students' needs and with the institution's goals? Might a teacher with an incremental conceptualization of intelligence conceivably be more effective with students having difficult learning histories? Such questions warrant consideration.

This study has important implications for those who teach students designated as non-achievers. Many say that learning in the schools is "going downhill" and that it is harder than ever to be a teacher. Whether or not this is reality is not the issue, but learning how best to teach all students is. Because underachievers are becoming college educated with the help of developmental education, it is in our best interest to find out more specifically what makes college developmental education successful. This study sheds light on one developmental teacher in one college reading classroom; however, there may be implications for others who desire to provide success for underachievers at any level of education. Further qualitative and quantitative research in this area, exploring faculty attitudes toward the concept of intelligence on a larger scale, is desperately needed to guide future practice.

References

Ames, C. (1992). Classrooms: Goals, structures, and student motivation. *Journal of Educational Psychology, 84* (3), 261-271.

Binet, A., & Simon, T. (1905). New methods for the diagnosis of the intellectual level of subnormals. *L'Annee Psychologique, 11,* 191-244.

Boylan, H.R., & Bonham, B.S. (1992). The impact of developmental education programs. *Research in Developmental Education, 9* (5),1.

Cattell, R.B. (1963). Theory of fluid and crystallized intelligence: A critical experiment. *Journal of Educational Psychology, 54* (1), 1-22.

Cattell R.B. (1971) *Abilities: Their structure, growth and action.* Boston: Houghton Mifflin.

Clark, C.M., & Peterson, P.L. (1986). Teachers' thought processes. In M.C. Wittrock (Ed.), *Handbook of research on teaching* (3rd ed.) (pp. 225-296). New York: Macmillan.

Collier, G. (1994). *Social origins of mental ability.* New York: John Wiley & Son.

Covington, M., & Omelich, C. (1979). Effort: The double-edged sword in school achievement. *Journal of Educational Psychology, 71,* 169-182.

Dweck, C.S. (1986). Motivational processes affecting learning. *American Psychologist, 41,* 1040-1048.

Dweck, C.S., & Bempechat, J. (1983). Children's theories of intelligence. In S. Paris, G. Olsen, & H. Stevenson (Eds.), *Learning and motivation in the classroom* (pp. 239-256). Hillsdale, NJ: Erlbaum.

Dweck, C.S., & Elliott, E.S. (1983) Achievement motivation. In E.M. Heatherington (Ed.), *Handbook of child psychology: Vol. 4, Socialization, personality, and social development* (pp. 643-691). New York: Wiley.

Dweck, C.S., & Leggett, E.L. (1988) A social-cognitive approach motivation and personality. *Psychological Review, 95,* 256-273.

Eisner, E. (1991). *The enlightened eye: Qualitative inquiry and the enhancement of educational practice.* New York: Macmillan.

Fjeldstad, F. (1994). *The thoughtful reader.* New York: Harcourt Brace.

Foster, H.M. (1994). *Crossing over: Whole language for secondary English teachers.* Fort Worth, TX: Harcourt Brace.

Gardner, H. (1983). *Frames of mind: The theory of multiple intelligences.* New York: Basic Books.

Garner, R. (1990). When children and adults do not use learning strategies. *Review of Educational Research, 60,* 517-530.

Goetz, J.P., & LeCompte, M.D. (1984). *Ethnography and qualitative design in educational research.* New York: Academic Press.

Good, T.L., & Brophy, J.E. (1991). *Looking in classrooms* (5th ed.). New York: Harper Collins.

Meyer, E. (1982). *The growth of biological thought.* Cambridge, MA: Belknap.

Nicholls, J., Patashnick, M., & Metteal, G. (1986). Conceptions of ability and intelligence. *Child Development, 57,* 636-645.

Paris, S.G., & Newman, R.S. (1990). Developmental aspects of self-regulated learning. *Educational Psychologist, 27,* 87-102.

Perry, W. (1968). *Forms of intellectual and ethical development in the college years.* NY: Holt, Rinehart, & Winston.

Pintrich, P.R., & Degroot, E.V. (1990). Motivational and self-regulated learning components of classroom academic performance. *Journal of Educational Psychology, 82,* 33-40.

Ryan, R.M., & Grolnick, W.S. (1986). Origins and pawns in the classroom: Self-report and projective assessments of individual differences in children's perceptions. *Journal of Personality and Social Psychology, 50,* 550-558.

Sherman, R.R., & Webb, R.B. (1988). Qualitative research in education: A focus. In R.R. Sherman & R.B. Webb (Eds.), *Qualitative research in education: Focus and methods* (pp. 2-21). New York: Falmer.

Slate, J.R., Jones, C.H., & Charlesworth, J.R., Jr. (1990). Relationship of conceptions of intelligence to preferred teaching behaviors. Action in Teacher Education: *Journal of the Association of Teacher Education, 12*(1), 25-29.

Spearman, C. (1927). *The ability of man.* New York: Macmillan.

Spradley, J. (1979). *The ethnographic interview.* New York: Holt, Rinehart, and Winston.

Spradley, J. (1980). *The participant observation.* New York: Holt, Rinehart, and Winston.

Sternberg, R.J. (1985). *Beyond IQ: A triarchic theory of human intelligence.* New York: Cambridge University.

Sternberg, R.J. (1988). A triarchic view of intelligence in cross-cultural perspective. In S.H. Irvine & J.W. Berry (Eds.), *Human abilities in cultural context* (pp. 60-85). New York: Cambridge University.

Vacca, R.T., & Vacca, J.A.L. (1993). *Content area reading* (4th ed.). New York: Harper Collins.

Wadsworth, B. (1989). *Piaget's theory of cognitive and affective development* (4th ed.). New York: Longman.

Weinberg, R.A. (1989). Intelligence and IQ. *American Psychologist, 44* (2), 98-104.

Winterowd, W.R. (1989). *The culture and politics of literacy*. New York: Oxford University.

Book Review

Martha Maxwell

MM Associates

Practical Approaches to
Using Learning Styles in Higher Education

Dunn, R. & Griggs, S. A. (Eds.) (2000)

Y̲ou will find a gold mine of information about how learning and teaching styles affect college students' performance in this book, including a road map to help you accommodate students' learning style strengths by comparing the major theories of learning styles, the instruments used to measure them, their research and applications and how to evaluate program effectiveness.

Twenty-five authors summarize their experience in using the Dunn Learning Styles Inventory (LSI) and the strategies they found useful in accommodating students with diverse learning styles in different institutions and many disciplines including education majors, doctoral students, counselors, and psychologists, as well those in business, liberal arts, engineering, health sciences, and nursing courses. Distance learning is also covered.

The book is designed to assist faculty in becoming knowledgeable about student learning styles and how to accommodate teaching styles to the preferred learning styles of their students. Of particular interest to learning specialists is the explanation of how to interpret individual learning styles profiles and help students design appropriate study strategies for specific course demands in order to maximize their learning. In other words, this book addresses teaching students how to teach themselves. You will surely find new ways to stretch your teaching styles as well as suggestions to help you and your colleagues in other disciplines learn about and effectively use teaching and learning styles in your teaching.

The book is based on The Learning Styles Inventory (Dunn, Dunn & Price, 1996a, 1996b), comprised of 21 elements (i.e., personal reactions that one concentrates on while learning new and difficult material), grouped in five areas: (a) reactions to the immediate environment, such as sound versus silence, bright versus soft lighting, and so on; (b) one's own emotionality (e.g., motivation, persistence); (c) sociological preferences for learning (e.g., alone, with peers, with either a collegial or authoritative adult); (d) physiological characteristics, perceptual strengths (e.g., auditory, visual, tactile, or kinesthetic), time of day energy levels, and so on; and (e) global versus analytical processing as demonstrated by correlations among factors such as sound, light, design, intake (e.g., snacking), sociological preferences.

Typically about 60% of teachers have analytical learning preferences and it may be hard for them to think of other ways to present course information to the 40% of the students who have global learning preferences. Many examples of how to structure learning situations to meet different student needs are described, so you are sure to find ideas that you can use to help students maximize their learning. In addition, there are two syllabi from an education course illustrating the differences in teaching the same course to students who have analytic learning preferences and to those who have global preferences.

The appendix contains two bibliographies—one of award winning research on the LSI and second, an annotated bibliography of LSI doctoral dissertations on college students. Numerous studies show students achieve higher grades and have better attitudes toward school when they study under conditions that are congruent rather than incongruent with their learning styles. I wonder how many fewer developmental students we would have in college today had their elementary and high school teachers been more knowledgeable about learning preferences and teaching styles and taught them how to adjust their learning strategies to their course demands.

References

Dunn, R., Dunn, K, & Price, G. (1996a). *The learning styles inventory (LSI)*. Lawrence, KS: Price Systems. (for freshmen and non-traditional college students).

Dunn, R. , Dunn, K. & Price, G. (1996b). *Productivity environmental preference survey*. Lawrence, KS: Price Systems. (A form of the LSI for high school students and working adults.)

Dunn, R., & Griggs, S.A. (Eds.) (2000). *Practical approaches to using learning styles in higher education*. Westport, CN: Bergin & Garvey.

CALL FOR SUBMISSIONS
2002 & 2003 NADE MONOGRAPHS

The NADE Monograph Committee is seeking submissions for the 2002 NADE monograph, *Developmental Education: Policy and Practice*. All submissions must be postmarked by May 15, 2001. Submissions for the 2003 NADE monograph (theme TBA) will be due by May 15, 2002. Submission will be reviewed on a rolling basis (i.e., as they are received). Early submissions are welcome. Submissions must comply with the *Publication Manual of the American Psychological Association* (4th ed.) and the "Guidelines for Authors" published on the following page. All authors are required to sign a nonduplication agreement. Send five copies of the manuscript, including title page and abstract on separate pages to:

Jeanne L. Higbee

Co-Editor, NADE Monograph Series

General College

University of Minnesota

333 Appleby Hall

128 Pleasant Street SE

Minneapolis, MN 55455

Phone: (612) 625-8015

Fax: (612) 625-0709

e-mail: higbe002@umn.edu

GUIDELINES FOR AUTHORS
NADE MONOGRAPH SERIES

To be considered for publication, manuscripts must comply with the following guidelines:

1. Manuscripts must be typewritten, double spaced, minimum one inch margins, regular type, preferably 12-point, no right justification. Do not use italics, bold, or special fonts.

2. The subject must be relevant to the monograph theme.

3. Manuscripts must not be duplications of previously published works or articles under consideration for publication elsewhere.

4. Manuscripts and reference style must be in accordance with the *Publication Manual of the American Psychological Association*, 4th edition. Submissions that do not comply with APA style will be returned to the author(s).

5. All authors must be members of the National Association for Developmental Education (NADE).

6. The title page must include the title of the article (not to exceed 12 words); the name and institutional affiliations of all authors; and the address, telephone numbers (office and home), FAX, and E-mail information, if available, for the lead author.

7. The second page should be an abstract of the manuscript, maximum 100 words.

8. The article should begin on the third page, and should not exceed 25 pages, including all references, figures, and tables.

9. Names and institutional affiliations must be omitted from the body of the manuscript. Where appropriate, these will be inserted following the blind review process.

10. Figures and tables must be camera ready, according to APA style, on 8 1/2" x 11" paper, one per page. Any figures, drawings, tables, etc., must be the original work of the author(s). Only figures and tables that are necessary support to the text will be published.

11. Only references cited in the manuscript may be included in the reference list. Care must be taken to attribute all quotations to their published sources. Direct quotes must be accompanied by citations, including page numbers. Citations and references must be provided for software, tests and measurements, videotapes, interviews, and personal correspondence, including via electronic mail. The author(s) are responsible for the accuracy of all citations and references.

12. The NADE Monograph will not publish acknowledgements except when required in recognition of an external funding source.

13. Manuscript authors must agree to abide by revision decisions made by the editorial board and editors.

14. Upon acceptance the author(s) will be responsible for making required revisions and resubmitting the manuscript on disk.